CW00434117

Everton FC

The First Kings
of Anfield

1890/91

Everton FC

The First Kings of Anfield
1890/91

Mark Metcalf

AMBERLEY

First published 2013

Amberley Publishing
The Hill, Stroud
Gloucestershire, GL5 4EP

www.amberley-books.com

Copyright © Mark Metcalf, 2013

The right of Mark Metcalf to be identified as the Author
of this work has been asserted in accordance with the
Copyrights, Designs and Patents Act 1988.

All rights reserved. No part of this book may be reprinted
or reproduced or utilised in any form or by any electronic,
mechanical or other means, now known or hereafter invented,
including photocopying and recording, or in any information
storage or retrieval system, without the permission in writing
from the Publishers.

British Library Cataloguing in Publication Data.
A catalogue record for this book is available from the British Library.

ISBN 978 1 4456 1800 5 (print)
ISBN 978 1 4456 1814 2 (ebook)

Typeset in 10pt on 12pt Sabon.
Typesetting and Origination by Amberley Publishing.
Printed in the UK.

Contents

Acknowledgements

Many thanks to Jim Fox, Roger Booth, Robert Boyling, George Orr, Tony Matthews and Tony Onslow for their help with this book.

Foreword

It's a pleasure and a privilege to be asked to write the foreword for this book on one of Everton's great sides and the first to capture the League title.

As someone who loves the history of our club, and football in general, I was fascinated to find out more about the players from this fabulous season, including Edgar Chadwick, who reminds me of my own favourite Everton forward, Alex Young. Both players were class acts, who in addition to scoring plenty of goals, also used their skills and movement to create a hatful of chances for their teammates.

In midfield, Alec Brady was the ball-playing genius we have come to expect in Everton sides ever since, while in defence Dan Doyle and Andrew Hannah were the perfect partnership as full-backs. At centre-half, Johnny Holt could combine both defence and attack, while up front the goalscoring skills of Fred Geary were complemented by the clever wing play of Alf Milward and Alex Latta.

As a result, the Everton 1890/91 side won the title in only the third season of League football, and in doing so ended Preston's dominance of the competition. This in itself should be enough for any Evertonian, but for football followers in general this book is to be recommended because it brings alive the style of football employed in its formative years, when there was no such thing as a goal net, penalties or even restrictions as to where 'keepers could handle the ball.

Brendan Barber

(Former General Secretary of the Trades Union Congress, an Everton fan since he saw the Toffees beat Nottingham Forest 6-0 on 7 October 1961, a match in which Alex Young – nicknamed 'the Golden Vision' for his silky touch – notched the sixth goal.)

Everton Football Club
1878–90

Everton Football Club was formed in 1878, and within a few short years had attracted a loyal and passionate following to its games at Stanley Park. Keen to become one of the leading football clubs, the club purchased, courtesy of self-made local businessman Mr Houlding, the lease on a piece of land near his home on Anfield Road in the summer of 1884. The Everton committee, along with players and supporters, then set to work. Working throughout the summer, they quickly enclosed the playing field and added a simple grandstand.

The first game played at the new ground on 27 September 1884 ended in a 5-0 win against Earlestown. Everton went on to play over 120 first-team games at Anfield during the four seasons they spent there, prior to joining the Football League. The club executive slowly developed the location until the capacity was about twenty thousand.

The ground was second to none in England, and helped Everton's election to the Football League. Alex Nisbet had represented the club at the famous Royal Hotel meeting in Manchester on Tuesday 17 April 1888, at which one of the key decisions was that visiting clubs would be guaranteed a sum of £15. Considering the crowds Everton were drawing, fulfilling this agreement was never going to be a problem. The new competition meant that from September 1888 onwards, sides would have a regular, competitive system of fixtures.

So it was that on Saturday 8 September 1888 Everton played their first League game. A 2-1 victory against Accrington was enjoyed by the highest crowd of the day at 10,000.

Any hopes, however, that the victory would be the springboard to a season of success quickly proved misplaced. By the end, Everton was well back in eighth place, twenty points behind runaway winners Preston North End. Goalscoring had proved a problem, and with just thirty-five the Toffees were the lowest scorers in the League. Home form had been decent, with sixteen points (two points for a win, one for a draw) from twenty-two, but on their travels only one victory and two draws had been earned from eleven matches.

Despite Everton's on-field difficulties, the crowds had continued to flock to Anfield and the funds generated made it possible for the club to look for better players. As an indication of the improvements to come, Alf Milward arrived from Marlow early in 1889. With Scotland continuing, until 1893, to resist the lure of paying footballers, the Everton committee were confident they could attract some of the best players in the world at the time to move south of the border. Alex Latta was signed from his local team Dumbarton Athletic – a fine athlete, who could play on either wing. He was a shipwright by trade and abstained from strong drink. Just twenty-two years old, he took up lodging with a Scottish family at Ellswater Street in the Walton district of Liverpool.

Fred Geary quickly joined him. Nottingham born, he was twenty-three years old when he joined Everton. He was slightly built, with a blistering turn of speed, and was signed from Nottingham Rangers. It was hoped he would solve Everton's goalscoring problem. Everton then signed a pair of classical tough-tackling and big-kicking full-backs. Danny Doyle was born in Paisley and began his playing career with Airdrie before moving to Edinburgh, where he played for Hibernians. In 1888, he joined Grimsby before completing the season at Bolton. In May he moved back to Edinburgh, from where he was persuaded to join Everton. Andrew Hannah was signed to partner Doyle at full-back. Born at Renton Dumbarton in 1864, Hannah had a successful spell with Renton before he moved south to join Everton. He was immediately appointed club captain.

Nineteen-year-old Charlie Parry was signed from the St Oswald club in Chester. Born at Llansilin in North Wales, Parry played for Oswestry before moving to Chester. He was a powerfully built and uncompromising young player, who weighed over 12 stone. Everton also signed locally born David Kirkwood.

Next to arrive was Alex Brady. A boilermaker by trade, Brady was born at Cathcart near Glasgow and joined Burnley from Partick Thistle in the summer of 1888. Brady scored seven goals in just twenty matches for the Turfites, mainly playing as a right-winger, before he left to join Sunderland in February 1889. He was transferred to Everton in November 1889, scoring two goals on his debut in an 8-0 victory against Stoke at Anfield.

The season proved to be much more successful and, despite a 5-1 hammering at Anfield in November by rivals Preston North End (a match that attracted a crowd of 18,000), Everton were just a point behind the reigning champions in late February. However, two defeats, both away, in the last four matches of the season proved just enough to allow the Deepdale side to win the title for the second consecutive season.

1889/1890 First Division Table

All sides played twenty-two matches. Two points for a win and one for a draw.

Team	Won	Drew	Lost	F-A	Points
Preston North End	15	3	4	71-30	33
Everton	14	3	5	65-40	31
Blackburn Rovers	12	3	7	78-41	27
Wolves	10	5	7	51-38	25
WBA	11	3	8	47-50	25
Accrington	9	6	7	53-56	25
Derby County	9	3	10	43-55	21
Aston Villa	7	5	10	43-51	19
Bolton Wanderers	9	1	12	54-65	19
Notts County	6	5	11	43-51	17
Burnley	4	5	13	36-65	13
Stoke City	3	4	15	27-69	10

Appearances: Chadwick 22, Doyle 22, Hannah 22, Milward 22, Parry 22, Holt 21, Latta 19, Geary 18, Smalley 17, Brady 13, Kirkwood 11, Bob Cain 10, George Farmer 10, Walter Cox 4, James Weir 3, Harry Hammond 1, James Jamieson 1, Charles Joliffe 1, Robert Jones 1, W. Orr 1, Frank Sugg 1.

Goalscorers: Geary 21, Milward 10, Chadwick 9, Latta 9, Brady 8, Parry 4, Holt 1, Orr 1.

The Everton Squad for the 1890/91 Season

The squad that had just missed out on the League title was strengthened before the 1890/91 season kicked off by the arrival of William Campbell from neighbouring Bootle. In September, as the season got underway, Patrick Gordon arrived from Scottish club Renton, preceding by a few weeks fellow Scotsman Tom Wylie, who had arrived from (Glasgow) Rangers. Then, in October, Hope Robertson arrived from Partick Thistle, and a month later another Bootle player, Andy Jardine, a goalkeeper, was signed. No fees were involved in the transfers and if Sir Frederick Wall, FA Secretary at the time, is correct, none was ever paid until Manchester City paid Preston North End £450 for right-back John McMahon in late 1902. Finally, just before Christmas, came the signing of another Scot, Alex Lochhead. All were to play some part in this most famous of seasons.

League Appearances

Edgar Chadwick 22 [10]
Described in Tony Matthews' *Who's Who of Everton* as 'a master strategist and dribbler', the Blackburn-born Chadwick was one of the great players of his generation. He and Alf Milward terrorised the right side of defences during the 1890/91 season, notching twenty-two goals between them including the three (Chadwick 1, Milward 2) in the single-goal victory at home to Accrington on Boxing Day that started a run of four consecutive home victories that eventually proved vital in the championship race. Chadwick played 300 times for the Everton first team, scoring 110 times. Capped seven times for his country, Chadwick had an unenviable record in the FA, playing in three FA Cup finals, including two with Everton, and losing the lot. Chadwick left Everton in 1899 and later played for Burnley, Southampton, Liverpool, Blackpool, Glossop North End and Darwen, where his long playing career ended in 1908 aged thirty-nine. He later managed on the Continent, and is generally recognised as

the first manager of the Dutch National team. After the First World War ended, he returned to his home town, Blackburn, and reverted to his original trade as a baker. He died in Blackburn on Valentine's Day 1942.

Alf Milward 22 [11]

According to Tony Matthews, Milward was 'a well-built, hard working and technically clever winger who contested every ball and had a knack of delivering a cross-field pass to perfection from up to 40 yards'. Milward scored twelve League goals during the season, including vital efforts in both of the Accrington games in 1890/91, fastening on to Edgar Chadwick's effort to drive home the winner in the away game in September, and then with Everton drawing 2-2 at Anfield, after losing five of the last nine, he blasted home an unstoppable shot from 25 yards to ensure two vital points on Boxing Day. Four times capped for England, he also played in three FA Cup finals, alongside his left-sided partner Chadwick, and lost all three including the 1900 final with Southampton. He died at Winchester on 1 June 1941.

Fred Geary 22 [20]

The Everton centre-forward scored eighty-six goals in ninety-eight first-team appearances, including twenty in the championship season. Twice capped for England, he scored a hat-trick on his debut against Ireland in March 1890. Geary was fast, brave, and a good header of the ball; he also possessed a lightning shot. Never afraid to have a shot at goal, Geary started the 1890/91 season in superb form, scoring in each of the first six matches. Geary prodded home a vital winning goal at Molineux in early December, before almost causing a riot by depositing the Wolves captain, Harry Allen, over the ropes around the touchline!

Geary signed for Liverpool in May 1895, where he made forty-five appearances in four seasons. He subsequently returned to Goodison Park as a groundsman. He died on 8 January 1955, aged eighty-six.

Johnny Holt 21 [1]

Lynchpin of the Everton side at centre-half, John Holt enjoyed ten years with the club, during which time he collected a League Winner's medal and was twice an FA Cup finalist. Although only 5 feet 5 inches tall, Holt was capable of some rough challenges, and none more so than during a fierce encounter with Bolton in October 1890. Capped ten times for England, Holt was a fantastic passer of the ball and, with boundless energy, was one of the stars of the early Everton sides.

Alec Brady 21 [9]

The first of many Everton inside-forwards who could bring others into play with deft, accurate passing. He had a fine eye for goal, and never more so than at home to Bolton in mid-October when he scored both goals. Brady formed a fine partnership with Alex Latta, and on leaving Everton in August 1891, he later helped Celtic win the Scottish Cup in 1892 and Sheffield Wednesday the FA Cup in 1896.

Dan Doyle [20]

Helped form a formidable full-back partnership with Hannah during the championship-winning season. Never the quickest of players, the Scotsman, who played eight times for his country, was a great reader of a forward pass, stepping in to clear with power and accuracy. Doyle caused uproar when he left Everton in the summer of 1891. After making forty-five first-team appearances, he moved back north to sign for Celtic, who were supposedly an amateur side, as professionalism had not yet been legalised in Scotland. Doyle performed with distinction for the Glasgow club, where he won the Scottish League title four times and also picked up a Scottish FA Cup winner's medal in 1892.

Doyle traded blows with Blackburn's Lofthouse during the home game in November 1890, and was the sort of player any side would like to have in their XI when the going gets tough.

Doyle died on 8 April 1918, and it is a sign of his importance to the development of Celtic that when the Celtic Graves Society was formed, it chose as their inaugural event in November 2010 to lay a headstone on Doyle's previously unmarked grave.

Andrew Hannah 20

His partnership with Dan Doyle was the best in the country in the two seasons the pair played together at Everton. Signed from Renton, where he gained two Scottish FA Cup winner's medals, Hannah went on to become the first man to captain both Everton and Liverpool, picking up a Second Division championship medal with the latter in 1893. A formidable opponent, Hannah was also capable of hitting the heavy balls of the late nineteenth century long distances, and it was from one of his long dropping shots that Hope Robertson followed up a save by the Sunderland 'keeper Ted Doig to strike home the only goal at Anfield in November 1890 for two vital points. Hannah died on 17 June 1940.

Dave Kirkwood 19 [1]

The Liverpool-born wing-half's fine 1890/91 season was to come to a disappointing end when he was made the scapegoat for Everton's FA Cup defeat at Sunderland and the penultimate League game at home to Preston North End. As a result, he was left out of the side for the final game at Burnley. Transferred at the end of the season, he later returned to Everton towards the end of 1891, before again leaving in March 1892 having made twenty-eight appearances in which he notched two goals.

Charlie Parry 13

A versatile player, Parry made ninety-four first-team Everton appearances, in which he struck home five goals. Playing at right-half, the Welshman, who won thirteen caps for his country, made a dramatic save in the last few minutes of the game at Aston Villa in October; this intervention proved priceless when Everton grabbed an equalising goal only minutes later to preserve their unbeaten start to the season. An injury saw him miss the later part of the 1890/91 season, but with eleven appearances he had already played a full part in Everton's greatest season to date.

William Campbell 13 [1]

He showed his versatility by playing at right-back, centre and left-half in the 1890/91 season for Everton. After scoring in his debut match away at West Brom, Campbell was one of the stars of the magnificent 5-0 victory in the third game of the season away at Bolton Wanderers.

Alex Latta 10 [4]

An outstanding outside-right, it was the loss of Latta, after he was injured in a friendly game against Third Lanark at the start of October, that threatened to derail Everton's charge for the title. Missing for much of the middle part of the season, Latta returned to reforge a deadly right-wing partnership with Alex Brady for the final five matches of the season. Against Burnley on 27 December, Everton were 2-1 down just before half-time when Latta scored a priceless equaliser before Brady drove Everton into the lead a minute later. The home side went on to win the match 7-3. Latta was capped twice by Scotland, and his pace and ability to shoot saw him complete his Everton career with a record of seventy goals in 148 first-team appearances.

Robert Smalley 1

The 'keeper made his final appearance for Everton in the away game at Ewood Park in November, but could do little to prevent a second consecutive defeat. Smalley had played in Everton's first-ever League game against Accrington in August 1888.

David Jardine 10

Jardine was signed for Everton from neighbours Bootle in November 1890. Thrown straight into the side for the Anfield game against Blackburn in November 1890, he remained in goal for the remaining League fixtures to help the Blues capture their first League title. Jardine made a vital save on the stroke of half-time at 2-2 during the Boxing Day game at home to Accrington, thus preventing the away side overturning what had been a two-goal deficit. It proved a turning point in Everton's season, as they went on to win 3-2 and moved back to the top of the table, where they remained to the season's end. Made a total of thirty-seven first-team appearances before moving to Nelson in May 1894.

Jack Angus 11

The 'keeper played his eleventh and final game of the season in the away game at Deepdale in November, performing with distinction to ensure Everton suffered only a two-goal defeat to a Preston side and demonstrating the sort of talents that had seen them win the Football League in its first two seasons. He was also between the sticks for the Blues when Sunderland knocked the side out of the FA Cup in early January, making it his final appearance for the club, as he was to die at the tender age of just twenty-four. On Saturday 8 August 1891, when spending his close season at home in Scotland at his father's on Deany, Leanhead, he was struck by typhoid fever. It gradually worsened and he died at 10 p.m. that night. He was a plumber by trade and unmarried.

The announcement in the *Liverpool Echo* on the following Monday came the same day as it was reported that Doyle and Brady had violated the principles of playing during the close season by turning out for Celtic against Cowlairs. This would result in them being cup-tied for Everton for the rest of the season. It is of interest that in the following weekend's *Football Echo* section there was an extensive examination of Doyle and Brady's motives, combined with some condemnatory letters, but not a thing about Angus's passing.

It's not recorded whether Angus showed signs of an illness before being replaced in goal, but Everton went out in November and signed David Jardine from Bootle as a replacement.

Duncan McLean 5

Accustomed to playing either left-back or left-half, McLean was another Scot that Everton signed from Renton. McLean played his best game away at Wolverhampton, but his five League games in the championship season included three defeats. He later played for Liverpool and won two international caps.

Patrick Gordon 3

Signed from Scottish club Renton in September 1890, the Scotsman made his debut the following month against Bolton, but played only twice more during the season. He later played at outside right in the Everton XI that lost to Wolves in the 1893 FA Cup final.

Jack Elliott 1

Elliott made a surprising debut, and his only appearance of the season, away at Notts County after Everton had been unable to find Hope Robertson, and after Alex Latta had reported injured on the morning of the match. He was to feature infrequently in the side, playing just fifteen times in five seasons.

Tom Wylie 4 [4]

Wylie might have played only four times in the season, but his signing in December 1890 from Glasgow Rangers was a shrewd move as Everton moved to strengthen the outside-right position in the absence of the injured Alex Latta. Performing with distinction in the side's narrow win at Molineux in early December, Wylie then hit four goals as Derby were thrashed 6-2 at home. Defeat at Sunderland was followed by another victory in his final game of the season against Accrington, before Latta returned from injury to play his part in the title run-in. Wylie made a total of twenty-one Everton appearances, scoring five goals, before signing for Liverpool in 1892. Wylie later won a Second Division winner's medal with Bury in 1895.

Hope Robertson 3 [1]

Signed from Partick Thistle in October 1890, and with Alex Latta out injured, he was thrown straight into the side at Ewood Park at outside-right. Although his presence failed to prevent a third consecutive defeat, Robertson, at centre-forward, played an important role in bringing Everton's mini-crisis to an end by notching the winner in the following game at home to Sunderland. After thirty-one appearances and two goals, he moved on to Bootle in November 1892.

Alex Lochhead [1]

The wing-half was pitched straight into the side for his debut match in the final vital game of the season at Burnley, after moving across the border from Third Lanark. It proved to be one of only six appearances for the Blues, as by the end of 1891 he had returned to Lanark.

Everton's League Opponents in 1890/91

Accrington	Founded in 1876. Football League founder member. Not to be confused with Accrington Stanley.
Aston Villa	Founded in 1874. Football League founder member. FA Cup winners in 1887.
Blackburn Rovers	Founded in 1874. Football League founder member. FA Cup winners in 1884, 1885, 1886 and 1890.
Bolton Wanderers	Founded in 1874. Football League founder member.
Burnley	Founded in 1881. Football League founder member.
Derby County	Founded in 1884. Football League founder member.
Notts County	Founded in 1862. Football League founder member.
Preston North End	Founded in 1881. Football League founder member. League championship winners 1888/89, 1889/90. FA Cup winners 1889.
Sunderland	Founded in 1879. Sunderland had replaced Stoke City at the end of the previous season and were looking forward to their first season of League football.
West Bromwich Albion	Founded in 1879. Football League founder member. FA Cup winners 1888.
Wolverhampton Wanderers	Founded in 1877. Football League founder member.

Organising the League

It was a Scot, William McGregor, who was responsible for first organising League football in England. In 1887, professionalism as a legal entity was only two years old and the Aston Villa committee man recognised that clubs needed a guaranteed source of income if they were to have the funds to pay players.

High-profile friendly matches and cup competitions were one thing, but on many occasions a growing band of fans was being forced to make do with one-sided contests or left frustrated at not knowing in advance who their side might be playing at the weekend. Football might have been, as it still is, a distraction from the cares of everyday life for fans, but that didn't mean they were content to watch uncompetitive matches.

With support from his fellow Villa committee members, McGregor set out to see which other clubs might join the Birmingham club in turning his new idea into reality. By early March the following year, he was confident enough to send a formal letter to five clubs: Blackburn Rovers, Bolton Wanderers, Preston North End, West Bromwich Albion and his own club, Aston Villa.

In this letter he suggested that clubs might overcome their current problems by ensuring that 'ten or twelve of the most prominent clubs in England combine to arrange home and away fixtures each season'. A conference was proposed to discuss the matter more fully and the five already invited to get involved were asked to suggest the names of other clubs who should be approached to join them. Bolton's secretary, John Bentley, put forward eight more names, although in the event two, Mitchell St George's from Birmingham and the amateur team Old Carthusians, never made it to the big kick-off in September 1888.

On the eve of the 1888 FA Cup final, held at the Oval between Preston North End and West Bromwich Albion, representatives of Aston Villa, Notts County, Blackburn Rovers, Wolverhampton Wanderers, Burnley, Stoke and West Bromwich Albion held a successful meeting. They then invited Preston North End, Everton, Accrington, Bolton Wanderers and Derby County to join them, in formalising affairs and arranging fixtures for the 1888/89 season at the Royal Hotel, Manchester on Tuesday 17 April 1888.

It is this meeting that marks the birth of competitive League football, and, historic as it might be, that didn't stop club representatives disagreeing amongst themselves! Even the name proved a problem, with McGregor's suggestion of Football Union being overruled in favour of Preston North End's William Sudell's preferred title of Football League. McGregor had wanted clubs to divide gate money, but delegates, who felt that a guaranteed sum of £15 for visiting clubs was a better option, rejected this idea. Egalitarianism had been quickly snuffed out in pursuit of profits. If McGregor was upset he didn't show it, and was duly elected as chairman of the new organisation, with Sudell taking on the role of treasurer and Harry Lockett that of honorary secretary.

Meanwhile, Sheffield Wednesday, Nottingham Forest and Halliwell, who claimed they were the second-best team in Lancashire, were all left disappointed when their applications to join the new League were rejected on grounds that it was impossible to find sufficient dates for any additional fixtures. So while the merits of some of the clubs were queried – Everton*, for example, were considered inferior to local rivals Bootle, Accrington's playing record was mixed and gates poor, Notts County had just experienced their worst season; and even three-time FA Cup winners Blackburn Rover's supremacy in the east Lancashire cotton town was coming under threat – those who had met on 17 April were happy to become a select band of pioneers. To their credit, they clearly knew what they were doing because eleven of them – Accrington being the exception – are all still playing in the Football/Premier League today.

The clubs were also clearly open to change, as they adopted rules that required the bottom four clubs to reapply for their place in the League in a re-election battle with non-League clubs who wished to join. With each League club allowed to cast four votes, Stoke became the first to lose out when they were replaced by Sunderland for the start of the 1890/91 season.

Here's how *the Cricket and Football Field* of 21 April 1888 reported developments:

A dozen Association clubs, who style themselves the pick of the talent, have joined hands for their own mutual benefit, apparently without a care for those unhappily shut out in the cold. The first public intimation of the hatching of the plan came on the eve of the FA Cup final, where clubs met at Anderton's Hotel and sent forth a circular ... They stressed they weren't against FA or the provincial associations and said there was nothing to stop other clubs forming a second League and they pointed to the Baseball Leagues in the USA where they have a dozen different leagues. They would work amicably with the second League and the four best in that would play the four worst in the Football League.

* Liverpool, in those early days, was well detached from the football hot-bed of East Lancashire, but was the largest town in terms of population in the Northern group. Why Mr McGregor invited Everton and not Bootle is now lost in the mists of time; the most likely explanation is that the Anfield ground was reserved for the sole purpose of association football. Bootle, like many other teams at the time, shared their ground with the local Cricket Club.

(Tony Onslow, *Everton FC: The Men from the Hill Country*)

Football in 1890

While a form of football has probably existed for as long as men have had feet with which to kick things, the game as we know it today was under 100 years old in 1890. Various forms of football had come into being in the major public schools during the second or third decade of the nineteenth century. Attempts to unify the different strands and establish a uniform system of rules were given a big boost when the Cambridge (University) Rules were drawn up in 1848. These were revised over the following decade. In November 1862, a match at Cambridge took place between Cambridge Old Etonians and Cambridge Old Harrovians on a level playing field, under a set of rules that, 150 years later, most football fans could recognise. Happily, the rules, which included eleven players on each side, worked, and the revised Cambridge rules of 1863 became the basis for the first laws of the Football Association (FA) that was formed on 26 October 1863.

Eight years later, on 11 November 1871, the first-ever matches in the longest running competitive football competition in the world took place when eight sides lined up in the FA Cup. Its success and that of the subsequent first international matches were the grounds on which the Football League could be established in 1888. Over this period, the tactics of football had altered significantly. While some sides continued to rely on the individual approach, in which each forward ran or dribbled with the ball as far as he could, before either losing it to a defender or having it taken from him by a frustrated colleague, profeesional teams were increasingly combining (or, in more modern terms, passing the ball from player to player) to create openings for an effort at goal. While Scottish side Queens Park are recognised as being the first side to master the art of 'letting the ball do the work', it was Preston North End who had, by 1888, started to 'scientifically' refine it. The change in approach meant it was out with a policy of just a couple of defenders, one half-back and seven forwards (with two centre-forwards), and in with team formations that began to combine both attack and defence with a 2-3-5 line-up of two full-backs, three half-backs and five forwards.

The centre-half did not, however, simply mark the opposing centre-forward, and had much greater freedom in which to assist other defending players, while principally supporting his forwards. Over time, it was usual for most sides to play their most creative player in this important position; this remained the case until rule changes in 1925 meant that players could now be onside if there were only two players between themselves and their opponents' goal rather than three.

The two full-backs rarely advanced up the field in 1888, and were selected for their ability to overpower the attacking forwards and for clearing the danger by kicking the ball well upfield, preferably accurately to the wings. With such heavy pitches this was not easy, and those who achieved the task were often warmly applauded.

At right- and left-half, players were required to provide passes to the forwards and help out in defence. As such, like the inside-forwards, they required great stamina, tackling ability, a never-say-die attitude, and skill in finding their forwards with an accurate pass. Some of the better ones could also be expected to chip in with a goal or two.

Wingers, of which every side would have two, were required to build partnerships with their respective inside-forwards, beat opponents either through pace or dribbling beyond them, and then create opportunities for the focal part of the attack, the centre-forward – the man to score the goals. How the latter did so wasn't important, and some were much better in the air, while others relied on pace over a few yards, anticipating a ball over the full-backs or worrying the life out of a 'keeper.

The names of those who managed to put the leather through the posts was cherished in the memory of all fans, and there were always more good forwards than good defenders, as the delight of scoring a goal far exceeds the pleasure of saving one. History does not tell of the men who saved goals, or even those who worked towards making them.

In 1888, new rules had restricted goalkeepers' use of their hands to their own half, the aim being to prevent them from joining in the attacks. What didn't change was that the men between the sticks could still be shoulder charged, with or without the ball, and there were some very rough challenges on them in 1890/91. Choosing whether to punch or catch a cross, or even a shot, often required a 'keeper to decide if he could subsequently get rid of the ball fast enough before an approaching forward clattered him. If he didn't, and was left injured, there was no such thing as a substitute 'keeper on the bench to replace him. In fact, there were no such things as substitutes until 1965. So if a player did get injured he was usually required, if possible, to limp out the match on the wing.

There was also no such thing as advertising on strips, and numbering on shirts was a good forty-plus years away. Meanwhile, the match ball could become a very heavy misshapen object when it became wet. Players' boots, largely adapted workmen's boots (and designed for strength with a permanent indestructible block toe), had studs hammered into the soles. Given the equipment, some of the play exhibited by the early giants of League football was extraordinary.

Pitches without adequate draining and very few markings bore no similarity to the fabulous billiard-table-like surfaces of the Football League today; they also had little grass on them, especially in the winter. Heavy rain brought puddles for the players to overcome, and on particularly rainy days the middle of the pitch would soon resemble a mud bath. This made it essential for teams to get the ball out to their wingers to attack the full-backs.

Deciding if any challenges in a game were in fact fouls was complex. It required a player to appeal for one, and then two umpires, one from each side, would decide whether to award a free-kick. Only if the umpires disagreed was the referee called upon to make the final decision. The end of the 1890/91 season was to bring radical change in the system, with the referee being given full control of the game, and the umpires being moved to the touchlines to become linesmen.

Match Reports in 1890/91

Early reporters faced a difficult job in reporting accurately on the games. The location from where they reported was not always conducive to following the play. There were no numbers on the jerseys of the players, and most had a 'short back and sides' haircut. This meant it was never easy to be certain who had made a last ditch tackle or scored a goal. This was especially so in the latter's case, as many were scored during fierce close to the goal tussles – or 'scrimmages' as they were then reported, amongst defenders and forwards.

Given that many reporters were relatively new to the game of football, and most only covered matches as part of their weekly work, then they also suffered from unfamiliarity with the players, particularly those playing for the opposition. It was hardly surprising then, that mistakes were made, with papers often reporting different scorers or simply the wrong ones. There was also no way of them gaining access to the players afterwards, especially for reporters working on Saturday night sports editions, to confirm facts and figures. All of this means the reader will find some inconsistencies in this book – for example, in some cases I have reported a scorer as taken from a paper or papers of the day that is at odds with the official club records compiled (in some cases) many decades later. As always, I have done my best to be objective with the 'facts'.

None of this should take away from the fine job that these early match reporters did in bringing to life the first League games in English and world football. To them and the early players we are all indebted; not that we always agree with their contents, of course, and in March 1891 Derby and Sunderland objected to a report of their match that appeared in *Athletic News*.

FA Committee member John Bentley promised to take matters up, as only he could, since he was the newspaper's assistant editor.

Fans unable to go to the games in 1890/91 relied on the written word to learn about on-field events, as there was no television coverage or action replays, radio commentary or after-match interviews with the club committees or managers responsible for team selection.

The reports had a certain symmetry to them, in that it was usual for them to start with news of who had won the toss, the winners generally preferring to take advantage of any wind or slope on the pitch in the first half – the aim being to build up a significant lead by half-time. There was also usually something on the weather conditions. This would indicate to the reader the pitch conditions, as with no such thing as specialist groundsmen or drainage systems, heavy rain would inevitably mean it was muddy, while ice would make it a problem for players to keep their feet. Accrington's ground was probably the best pitch in 1890 – a factor no doubt influenced by it also serving as a first-class cricket ground.

In 1890, specialist photographic equipment capable of capturing moving images had not yet been invented. On major occasions, such as FA Cup semi-finals or key League matches, some papers might bring the action alive by employing an artist to draw the winning goal or a section of the ground and crowd. Such was the case for a number of Everton's games in 1890 and 1891.

Some 'Facts'

The first football paper is believed to be *The Goal,* printed in November 1878. The *Athletic News* was first printed in 1880, and by the mid-1880s a number of towns and cities had their own Saturday night 'football specials'. The author's personal favourite is Bolton's 'Buff' that was officially called *Cricket and Football Field,* and which could be bought across many parts of Lancashire by 7.30 p.m. on Saturday evenings. The first time reporters could telephone in their reports to their papers is believed to be for the 1886 FA Cup final replay between Blackburn Rovers and West Bromwich Albion, played at the Derby Racecourse.

Professionalism

All of the clubs that formed the Football League in 1888 contained a majority of professional, paid players. In the quarter of a century since the FA had been formed, football had changed from being a game once played for keen enjoyment and keeping fit. No longer were teams composed of representatives of the best players in a team or a district. In order to find funds to pay a groundsman and for rent of a ground, clubs had placed fences and constructed stands and terraces in order to charge for entry to matches.

Increased crowds, particularly for FA Cup games, had brought surplus funds into clubs. These could be used to pay the better local players for not working, thus at a stroke removing the advantage many amateurs from better-off backgrounds held by having more time in which to practise their skills and keep fit, as well as offering payment to better players from far and wide.

Not everyone, though, was happy at such arrangements, and it took a struggle to achieve professionalism in the game of football. Darwen are believed to be the first to employ professionals when Jimmy Love and Fergus Suter of Partick Thistle helped the East Lancs side become the first from the north to reach the last eight of the FA Cup in 1879, where they only lost out after three matches to eventual winners Old Etonians.

By 1883, Blackburn Olympic had won the FA Cup with a side largely composed of players being paid to play, and yet that same year Accrington were expelled from the FA for paying players. Then in 1884 Preston North End were disqualified from the FA Cup after admitting they were paying players in order to compete with Blackburn Rovers, including Fergus Suter, who won the competition for three consecutive seasons starting in 1884.

In response, thirty-seven clubs that were determined to play professionally set up the British Football Association as a rival to the Football Association. This threat of secession did the trick, with the FA agreeing to legalise professionalism on 20 July 1885. All professional players had to register with the FA, had to have been born or lived for two years within a 6-mile radius of the ground (these residential qualifications were removed in May 1889), and those seeking to play for more than one club in a season had to gain the organisation's permission.

Despite the changes, not everyone was happy, and for a long time after, professionals chosen to represent England at international level could expect to be handed a tight-fitting, often coarse shirt, while in newspaper reports it was usual to give only their surname instead of also including their initials as was the case for the amateur player.

Professionalism saw all the major clubs seek to induce players from Scotland to join them. Football over the border was considered to be superior due to a greater willingness to emphasise teamwork rather than rely on individuals.

By the time the Football League started, the FA Cup had been won for seven consecutive seasons by clubs with professional players. The days of the amateur were coming to an end, although for a number of seasons afterwards they continued to make up the bulk of the England international side selected by the FA committee.

While players were often referred to as labourers, they did not receive protection under the Employers Liability Act 1880, and it was not to be until 1907 that the Football League established the Football Mutual Insurance Federation. Even then, the matter was left to the club and it took another five years for it to be compulsory for clubs to insure their players. Meanwhile, clubs also attempted to extend their authority over the personal lives of players – especially when it came to drink!

Despite the better wages, a footballer's life was close to the unskilled masses because of his constant insecurity. Injury could halt a promising career at any point, while contracts were subject to yearly renewal for all but a select few.

The Everton players were paid as follows in the 1890/91 season:

Hannah – £3 a week all year plus £50 as a present.
Doyle, Holt, Latta, Brady, Geary and Chadwick – £3 a week all year.
Milward, Angus, Kirkwood – 50s (£2.50) during the season and £2 during summer.
Campbell – £3 a week during playing season and 30s (£1.50) during summer.
Smalley, Parry – £2 a week all year.
G. Dobson – 30s all year.
McGregor – 35s (£1.75) during season and £1 in summer.
R. Jones – 15s (75p) all year.
G. Martin – 10s (50p) during playing season.
J. J. Murray – 5s (25p) all season.

The average male wage in the UK in the 1890s was 20s (£1) for a working week of fifty-four hours. This made the Everton professional footballer considerably better off than his working-class peers in the Liverpool community. However, changes were afoot that would restrict a player's ability to increase their income by moving to another club for higher wages. Starting in the 1893/94 season, once a player was registered with a Football League club, he could not be registered with any other club, even in subsequent seasons, without the permission of the club he was registered with. This applied even if the player's annual contract with the club holding his registration was not renewed after it expired. The club did not have to play him and, without a contract, he was not entitled to a wage. Yet, if the club refused to release his registration, the player was not allowed to play for any other Football League club. The player registration system came to be known as the 'retain and transfer' system. The situation became even worse for players when maximum wage legislation in 1901/02 restricted wages to £4 a week.

For some players, there were also opportunities to profit from the growing commercial appeal of the game. George Dobson was an agent for R. Mercer of Bolton (which was famous for manufacturing football goods) for many years.

Another Evertonian, Frank Sugg, who played for the club in the 1888/89 season, was even more successful. He was a brilliant all-round sportsman who also took part in weightlifting, swimming, shotput, billiards and rifle shooting, as well as playing football and cricket. He opened a sports shop in Liverpool with his younger brother Frank in 1894. Over the years more shops were added and, although the brothers split commercially in 1927 they both remained in business until they died within days of each other in 1931. The final link with the business only came to an end in January 2001, when Sugg Sport closed its eleven sports stores with the loss of 118 jobs.

Captaincy

The role of captain in football is an important one. This was especially so in 1890/91, as most teams were selected by a club committee (later known as directors) rather than a single manager. In addition with no such thing as dugouts – the first being at Pittodrie, Aberdeen, during the 1920s – those responsible for team selection would generally be seated in the main stand and as such some distance away from the pitch. There was also only a five-minute interval, which on occasions was not even taken if the weather was poor and there was a chance of it becoming dark before the intended end of the match.

All this increased the captain's role, and a good one would look to change player's positions during the match if he felt it would help his side. James Brown was one of the best-known captains of the 1880s, and he held the FA Cup aloft for Blackburn Rovers in 1884, 1885 and 1886.

The captain of the Aston Villa side that won the 1887 FA Cup was Archibald Hunter, who played for the club for many years until he suffered a heart attack when playing against Everton on Merseyside on 4 January 1890. Never fully recovering, the player known as 'The Old Warhorse' died four years later at the age of just thirty-five. Hunter had become the first player to score in every round of the 1886/87 FA Cup, including the final in which West Brom were beaten 2-0. Hunter was a clever player with a commanding personality, and in 1890 the *Birmingham Weekly Mercury* published a series of his thoughts in *Triumphs of the Cricket and Football Field*. In this he said:

> I think a captain should make it one of the first rules that every man should get into the habit of defending his position. I greatly dislike to see men scampering wildly over the field, leaving their places unprotected, forgetting their own particular duty and doing another man's work.

After moving from Ayr to Birmingham, Hunter had been persuaded to join Aston Villa in 1876 because a 'brother Scot', Mr George Ramsay, was the captain of the side. According to Graham McColl in his book, *Aston Villa: 1874–1998*:

The influence of Ramsay, then Hunter, led Villa to develop an intricate passing game, a revolutionary move for an English club in the late 1870s. It was a style of play pioneered by Queen's Park in Scotland. This type of sophisticated teamwork had rarely been employed in England.

Ramsay held the position of club secretary at Villa from 1884 to 1926.

Why Saturday Afternoon?

The third Football League season got underway on Saturday 6 September 1890, with a kick-off time of mid-afternoon.

The day of the week, starting time and period of the year were all-important. The importance of religion in everyday life at the time was underlined in rule 25 of the Football Association. This stated that 'matches shall not be played on Sundays within the jurisdiction of the Association'. Unable to utilise the one day in the week when the vast majority of people would not be at work, the game's authorities had rightly chosen the next best day, Saturday, where, starting in the 1840s, there had been a significant number of changes made to the working week.

Increased wages, in part the result of trade union agitation, especially amongst industrial workers, meant that in Nottingham many hosiery workers now had regular Saturday half-holidays and Lancashire builders stopped at 1 p.m. In addition, many of the more traditional craft trades were less rigid about hours of work and could, if they wished, take Saturday afternoon off to go and watch football. All of which meant that crowds tended to be socially mixed, as was never the case for those behind the organising of football clubs, with a survey of the occupation of 740 men who were directors of professional clubs from 1888 to 1915 showing an overwhelming majority who were middle class.

By starting the season in September clubs, many of which had started life sharing grounds with the local cricket club (and in 1890 Accrington, Derby and Notts County were still doing so) could be assured of a pitch on which to play on. So mid-afternoon it was. Of course, with no such thing as floodlights it also proved important to ensure games, especially in the middle of winter, got started early enough to finish before darkness engulfed the pitch.

The Championship Season

Great Start
League Game 1
Saturday 6 September 1890
West Bromwich Albion 1(Pearson) *v.* Everton 4 (Geary 2, Brady, Campbell)
Venue: Stoney Lane
Attendance: 5,600

WBA: J. Reader, H. Green, S. Powell, E. Horton, C. Perry, J. Bayliss, W. Bassett, S. Nicholls, F. Dyer, T. Pearson, H. Roberts.

Everton: J. Angus, A. Hannah, D. Doyle, D. Kirkwood, J. Holt, W. Campbell, A. Latta, A. Brady, F. Geary, E. Chadwick, A. Milward.

Everton's first League game of the 1890/91 season saw them go back to Stoney Lane. This was the ground on which a 4-1 final-day defeat at the end of the previous campaign had resulted in PNE not needing to worry about beating Notts County five days later to take the Division One championship for the second time. Scorers for WBA had been G. Evans with two, Pearson and Wilson. Geary had struck the Everton reply. More than any side at the time, WBA played the wing game with Perry, in particular, continuously seeking out Billy Bassett.

Only five of the 1889 WBA successful FA Cup-winning side were on display in the opening day's fixture of the 1890/91 season. One of them, Tom Pearson, was the first player to score a League hat-trick for the Baggies, notching four goals against Bolton on 4 November 1889. Pearson was his side's top League scorer during the first five seasons in the Football League. There was, however, no place for G. Evans, who had scored twice against Everton during the previous campaign.

The game was to produce a complete reversal in fortunes, previously defeated Everton this time winning 4-1 with two goals from Geary and efforts from Brady and Campbell against just a single Pearson reply.

It was, however, the Baggies who were the first to show in the match, and after Billy Bassett and Sammy Nicholls both had dangerous runs checked by Dan Doyle, Pearson finished off a fine pass from Bassett to leave Angus with no chance.

However, on a beautiful summer's afternoon, and with the sun shining directly into their eyes, it wasn't long before the home side were struggling to contain an Everton side determined to get back on level terms as quickly as possible. Chadwick shot narrowly wide and had another shot blocked before Campbell and Brady were both denied by last-gasp tackles.

Everton's pressure continued with Brady and Geary both shooting just wide, before some tricky play down the Everton right by Brady and Latta resulted in the ball being pulled back for Geary to equalise. Try as they might, the West Bromwich side could hardly get out of their own half as Everton showed great attacking play, but failed to earn the leading goal they deserved, leaving the game tied at 1-1 at half-time.

Following the five-minute interval, Joe Reader in the home goal punched the ball over as the second period started as the first ended with Everton on the attack. Geary might have done better with a close range effort, but with Milward and Chadwick carving open the Throstles' defence, Geary's second goal made it 2-1 to a Toffees side now in full flow.

Bassett might have equalised, but Angus was able to get a hand on his shot, and as it bounced towards the line Doyle was back to hack it forward where an alert Geary dashed forward and forced Reader to save at the expense of a corner. When this was sent over, Campbell gave the scoreline a more accurate reflection by heading home to put Everton 3-1 up.

Everton were now playing superbly, and it was no surprise when they added a fourth.

> The home side at the time were entirely beaten, the combination of the Evertonians being irresistible, and Brady from a short-range effort was easily able to notch the fourth point. Shot after shot was banged on, but they were repelled by Reader, who was proving himself a guardian of no mean ability.
>
> (*Liverpool Courier*)

The match thus ended with an emphatic victory for an Everton side intent on putting down a marker for the rest of the season. The away side had started the match poorly, and yet after failing behind, Everton had refused to be intimidated. Retaining their composure, they had soundly beaten a WBA side that had started the match so confidently.

Elsewhere
Bolton 4 Notts County 2
Accrington 1 Burnley 1
Derby 8 Blackburn Rovers 5
Wolves 2 Aston Villa 1

West Bromwich Albion– Stoney Lane

Albion had moved into Stoney Lane in the summer of 1885 and were to stay fifteen seasons before moving to their current ground, the Hawthorns. Converting the ground into a suitable home saw the field returfed and a wooden grandstand, affectionately known as the Noah's Ark Stand, was built with covering for 600 spectators in the middle and space for a further 1,500 at the ends.

On the opposite side, the uncovered ground was covered in ash, which eventually was raised back to give everyone a good view. The first season tickets at Stoney Lane cost 5s (25p), the usual admission charge being 6d (2.5p).

The first game played there was against The Third Lanark Rifle Volunteers from Glasgow on the 5 September 1885. Albion won 4-1. Albion's record victory, a 12-0 defeat of Darwen, was recorded at Stoney Lane in 1892, and the ground saw the most successful period in the club's history.

Famous Opponents

Ezra Horton – right-half: Known as 'Ironsides', he was as tough as they come, never flinched, was always aggressive in his approach and very sporting. A West Bromwich-born player (1866), he made eighty-three appearances for the club between 1882 and 1891, playing in successive FA Cup finals of 1886, '87 and '88, gaining a winner's medal in the latter. He skippered the team at times, and played in each of Albion's first thirty-six FA Cup games (from 1883). In fact, he starred in Albion's first FA Cup tie and the club's first-ever League game. He died in West Bromwich in 1939.

Charlie Perry – centre-half: A brilliant defender, cool and efficient who served Albion for twelve years as a player (1884–96) and then as a director for six (1896–1902). He won three England caps, played in four international trials, appeared twice for the Football League and in all made 219 first-class appearances for the Baggies (sixteen goals scored). He lined up in four FA Cup finals, 1886, '87, '88 and '92, gaining winner's medals in the last two. Born in West Bromwich in 1866, Charlie died in the same town in 1927. His brothers Tom and Walter also played for Albion's League side.

Fine Home Victory

League Game 2
Saturday 13 September 1890
Everton 5 (Geary 2, Milward 2, Chadwick) *v.* Wolverhampton Wanderers 0
Venue: Anfield
Attendance: 8,000

Everton: J. Angus, A. Hannah, D. Doyle, D. Kirkwood, J. Holt, W. Campbell, A. Latta, A. Brady, F. Geary, E. Chadwick, A. Milward.

Wolves: W. Rose, R. Baugh, C. Mason, A. Fletcher, H. Allen, A. Lowder, D. Wykes, A. Worrall, S. Thomson, H. Wood, J. Bowdler.

Wolverhampton Wanderers came to Anfield for Everton's first home game of the season on the back of a 2-1 opening-day victory against near neighbours Aston Villa. Manager Jack Adenbrooke had strengthened the Molineux attack by signing Sammy Thomson, a member of the Preston side that had won the previous two League championship titles, and he scored his sides first against Villa.

Overworked Turnstiles

Although the Everton club executive had invested heavily in new turnstiles, there were not enough to allow all spectators to gain entry before kick-off for a match that was played in boiling hot conditions.

Thomson for Wolves got the match underway, but they were soon forced onto the defensive and Billy Rose had to be alert to grab hold of a speculative long-range Campbell effort. Kirkwood, in defence for Everton, then earned a huge cheer after he took the ball away from John Bowdler as the Wolves man rushed forward.

Rose was grateful when a Latta shot hit the bar and he was able to pounce on the loose ball, and the Everton player was then twice denied by the 'keeper with shots that on another day may have opened the scoring. When Milward scored there were huge cheers, but these were stifled when the effort was disallowed for what appeared to reporters to be offside, although no one was actually too sure. Milward did, however, make it 1-0 when, from what appeared to be an offside* position, he forced the ball past Rose just before the half-time break.

It took the home side less than a minute of the second half to double their lead, Brady's splendid run being finished off by Geary. It was soon 3-0 when Latta crossed, and although Rose saved Geary's powerful header, Milward came forward to send the ball between the posts and hats from spectators up into the air in celebration. They were soon being thrown back up, as within less than a minute it was 4-0, Chadwick beating Rose.

With eighty minutes gone, Wolves finally threatened Angus in the Everton goal who kicked Thomson's shot clear. It was only a temporary reprieve, as just before the end Chadwick was able to make it 5-0, after which the sound of the referee's whistle on ninety minutes must have come as a welcome relief to all of the players, by now baking in the heat.

*It could have been that the ball had come off a defender first, as in 1890 an attacking player would be placed on-side if the ball came to him from an opponent. At the same time, a 'goal' was more likely to be disallowed if a forward, standing behind the defenders, obstructed the view of the 'keeper. It goes without saying that the offside rule was just as contentious in the first seasons of League football as it is today.

A Faultless Half-Back Display

After their opening victory away at Wolves' neighbours West Bromwich, this fine victory by Everton again showed they were now ready to challenge Preston North End's grip on the Division One championship. Scoring five goals was some feat, but so too was keeping out a forward line such as Wolves, and the newspapers all commented favourably on how well the Everton half-back line-up had played. They had broken up the away side's attacks with quick speedy tackles and anticipation of passes and then fed the ball quickly to their own forwards.

Offside Law

The term 'offside' derives from the military term 'off the strength of his side', and any soldier found to be so is denied pay and rations until placed 'back on the strength of his unit' by someone other than himself. As such, an offside player is termed to be 'out of play'. The origins of the offside rule descend from the game's original Rugby roots, in which forward passes were not allowed and anyone standing in front of the ball was offside. As it didn't take long to recognise that for the game of football to flow freely it needed forward passes, then there was also the need for a properly structured offside law.

On 1 December 1863, the first set of fourteen Football Association rules were drawn up and over the following three years the rules were revised such that by 1866 the offside rule was as follows:

> When a player has kicked the ball, any one of the same side who is nearer to the opponents' goal line is out of play and may not touch the ball himself nor in any way whatever prevent any other player from doing so until the ball has been played unless there are at least three of his opponents between him and their own goal but no player is out of play when the ball is kicked from behind the goal line

The above has, in essence, formed the basis of the offside law ever since, with the following exceptions:

In 1907 offside was limited to the opponent's half of the half of field of play only.

In 1925/26, after the International Board had accepted a proposal by the Scottish FA, it was decided to reduce from three to two the number of defenders who could place an attacker offside.

Elsewhere
Aston Villa 3 Notts County 2
Blackburn 0 Accrington 0
Bolton 3 Derby 1
Sunderland 2 Burnley 3
PNE 3 WBA 0

Colour Clash
Monday 15 September 1890
Sunderland 3 *v.* Wolves 4

This game was the first colour clash in League football, with both sides playing in red-and-white striped shirts. It was resolved that the home club should thereafter change its colours. To avoid future clashes, home clubs were instructed to have a set of white shirts available for emergencies and to register their colours with the League at the beginning of each season. Today's ruling that away clubs change their strip in the event of a clash was introduced in 1921. The colour of socks had to be registered after 1937.

Huge Away Following Enjoy a Brilliant Performance
League Game 3
Saturday 20 September 1890
Bolton Wanderers 0 *v.* Everton 5 (Geary 2, Milward 2, Latta)
Venue: Pikes Lane
Attendance: 12,000

Bolton Wanderers: J. Parkinson, J. Somerville, D. Jones, A. Paton, A. Barbour, R. Roberts, J. Davenport, J. Brogan, J. Cassidy, J. McNee, J. Munro.

Everton: Everton: J. Angus, A. Hannah, D. Doyle, D. Kirkwood, J. Holt, W. Campbell, A. Latta, A. Brady, F. Geary, E. Chadwick, A. Milward.

Referee: Mr W. H. Hope

'Liverpudliana' by Richard Samuel in *Cricket and Football Field*: 'I doubt if there is anything in the most brilliant history of the great Preston team to equal the performance of the Everton club during the first month of the season.'

Second against first, with both teams having won their opening two games, had raised excitement amongst the growing number of followers of both these sides. It meant that the gate of 12,000 at Pikes Lane was nearly treble that of the previous season, when the home side had won a thrilling game 4-3. The Lancashire & Yorkshire Railway Company had done its best to swell the numbers by issuing special tickets for a radius of 15 miles around Bolton, and also putting on additional excursions from the 'city of ships' as was.

With heavy rain overnight and showers falling all day the pitch, with its thick grass, made the going heavy for the players, especially as the game moved into the second half. A good number of councillors had joined the large ranks of Evertonians at the match, that started with Bolton pressing and Doyle needed to be in quickly to block Jimmy Munro as he shaped to shoot when well placed. Bolton were then foiled by a good Angus save, before Latta might have given the away side the lead, only to be denied by a beautiful save from James Parkinson.

The game was living up to its pre-match poster billing as 'the fight for the top place', but on eight minutes it was the away side that struck the opening goal. It came when, following good play between Kirkwood and Geary, the ball was directed towards Latta, who this time gave Parkinson no chance. This success was, of course, warmly appreciated by the Everton contingent.

Buoyed by taking the lead, Everton pushed forward. Three corners were scrambled clear by the desperate Bolton defence and when the home side did manage to relieve the pressure they found Campbell and Holt in stubborn mood.

Geary should then have done better when Latta sent him clear of the Bolton defence, hitting his shot well wide. The mistake was soon to be forgotten, however, as Milward made it 2-0 after Chadwick had created space for the outside left to beat Parkinson.

Wanderers were stung, and they pressed urgently, but again the Everton half-backs were not to be broken, and when the pressure was relieved a Geary cross could only be blocked by Dai Jones and as the ball landed Milward hit it powerfully past a bewildered Parkinson to give Everton a 3-0 half-time lead.

When play resumed, Bolton was grateful to be playing with the wind, yet this failed to prevent a fine interchange of passes down the Everton left between Chadwick and Milward to set up Geary for a shot that Parkinson should probably have saved as it sailed into the net to make it 4-0.

There was by now no doubt who would be top of the League at the end of the game, especially as the Everton rearguard was playing so well that Angus was only occasionally troubled in goal, although Jimmy Cassidy should have done better when left with a one-on-on with the 'keeper, only for the Bolton centre-forward to fluff his opportunity.

There were some heavy shoulder charges by both sides as the ball became stuck in the mud, and while in the 1890s players would be reluctant to go down injured for fear of encouraging their opponents, a number were forced to seek treatment. Everton's fifth goal came after a remarkable run by Chadwick, who carrying the ball almost 50 yards, across mud and water, found Milward who centred, and found Latta rushing in to hammer home.

The score had been 5-0 – not flattering for the away side – leaving the Match Reporter from *Cricket and Football Field* to conclude,

> Everton had played fine football and were very quick on the ball, their shooting being a strong point. They had also had to overcome a difficult pitch that had made passing extremely difficult, all of which boded well for the remainder of the season.

It had been a great start to Everton's third League season and they stood proudly at the top of the League.

Table

Everton	3	3-0-0	14-1	6
Burnley	3	2-1-0	6-4	5
PNE	2	2-0-0	6-1	4
Bolton	3	2-0-1	7-8	4

Elsewhere
Burnley 2 Aston Villa 1
Derby 1 PNE 3
WBA 0 Sunderland 4
Notts County 5 Accrington 0

Pikes Lane

In 1888, Bolton's home games were played at Pikes Lane. In 1881, Bolton had moved there after wandering around seeking a permanent pitch since being formed seven years earlier. This was a notoriously muddy ground situated at the foot of a hill. Then a cotton manufacturing town, the population of Bolton was just over 90,000, making it big enough to support a successful Football League team.

The first season of League football saw dressing rooms installed at Pikes Lane, which was last used at the end of the 1894/95 season. The ground hosted the first Inter-League game on 11 April 1892 when Football League drew 2-2 with Scottish League. Housing now covers the site of Pikes Lane.

David 'Dai' Jones

Capped fourteen times for Wales, Dai Jones could play in either full-back position, where his strong tackling and ability to kick with either foot made him a big favourite at Bolton, where he played for the first ten League seasons making 228 League and twenty-seven FA Cup appearances, scoring eight goals. Captain of the Wanderers side that lost out to Notts County in the 1894 FA Cup final, Jones later won a Second Division championship medal with Manchester City, for whom he played 114 times.

Four in a Row After Tough Encounter

League Game 4
Saturday 27 September 1890
Accrington 1 (Whitehead) *v.* Everton 2 (Geary, Milward)
Venue: Thorneyholme Road
Attendance: 5,000

Accrington: T. Hay, R. McDermid, J. Nisbet, M. Sanders, G. Haworth, J. Tattersall, P. Gallacher, J. Whitehead, J. Barlow, T. Thomson, A. Barbour.

Everton: J. Angus, A. Hannah, D. Doyle, D. Kirkwood, J. Holt, W. Campbell, A. Latta, A. Brady, F. Geary, E. Chadwick, A. Milward.

Everton's fourth League game of the season was away at Accrington Football Club. Accrington played their home matches at Thorneyholme Road, home of Accrington Cricket Club.

Accrington had finished seventh and sixth in the first two League seasons, and are not to be confused with local rivals Stanley. Accrington were to go out of business in 1896, when following relegation in 1892/93 they left the Football League after refusing to play in the Second Division. The side Everton faced in September 1890 included five-times-capped England international George Haworth, who was an FA Cup winner with Blackburn in 1885. Inside-forward Jimmy Whitehead was also later capped for England in 1893.

Considering that both Burnley and Blackburn were also at home, the crowd of 5,000 was a good one, and included an estimated 2,000 from Liverpool.

Having won the toss, George Haworth, the Accrington captain, chose to force Everton to kick with a strong sun shining in their eyes. Yet it was the away side that showed first, and the Accrington 'keeper Tom Hay had to be alert to grab an early shot, before J. M. Barlow replied forcing Angus to get down low to smother the ball. Holt then appeared to have given Everton the lead, but the cheers of the away fans were stilled when he was ruled offside after beating the 'keeper.

Jimmy Tattersall and Tommy Thomson then tried their luck, but both shots failed to trouble the Everton 'keeper. When Everton launched a series of high crosses, Hay punched both away, to the acclaim of the home faithful in the crowd. Haworth, around who, much of Accrington's play was centred, might have done better with a shot from just outside the penalty area before Jimmy Whitehead hit a fierce shot that flew past Angus to make it 1-0 to the home side.

Soon after there was even more joy for Accrington when Gallacher appeared to have put the ball between the posts, only for the referee, Mr Lackett, in the absence of confirmation of a goal net (*see following page*), to decide it had gone outside the posts. To the disappointment of 'the Reds' he awarded a goal-kick. To add insult to injury, the away team then almost immediately equalised when, with Hay down, following a heavy aerial challenge that left him pole axed, Geary scored. When half-time arrived, the score remained 1-1.

It was the away side that started more impressively when the game recommenced. Doyle had a shot that passed wide before Latta beat the 'keeper, only to be left disappointed when his effort was ruled out for offside. Yet Everton were not to be denied, and although Hay made a great save to deny Chadwick, the loose ball was pushed back past him by Milward to the rapturous applause of the Evertonians in the crowd.

With Everton now in full flight, Accrington was forced to defend desperately, but when the home side did manage to get forward they almost snatched a draw, only for Angus to save a hard shot from Thomson. It was, though, the away side that took the honours by finishing the match winners by two goals to one. It had been a hard-fought match and Everton had snatched two valuable points.

Elsewhere
Aston Villa 0 V. WBA 4
Blackburn 2 Wolves 3
Burnley 3 Sunderland 3
PNE 1 Bolton 0
Notts County 2 Derby County 1

Thorneyholme
The pitch at Thorneyholme Road Cricket Ground was possibly the best in the Football League in 1888. For instance, it was flat and therefore, unlike in reports from other grounds, there are no references to sides kicking off 'up the hill'.

Pitches in 1888/89 had very few markings on them. Boundary lines had been introduced in 1870, before which only two goalposts and four corner flag posts were the order of the day. In 1888, the goal area was two arcs of a 6-yard radius from the goalposts, and when the penalty kick was introduced it could be taken anywhere along the newly introduced line of 12 yards. In 1902, the penalty box was introduced, along with the penalty spot and goal area. The 'D' on the edge of box was introduced in 1937/38 to ensure all players were 10 yards away from a penalty taker.

George Haworth
Haworth signed for Accrington in 1882 and played for the club for more than decade. In 1884/85, Haworth also represented Blackburn Rovers and was a

member of the team that beat Scottish side Queens Park in the FA Cup final. A fine captain and defensive leader, he won five England caps in the period between 1887 and 1890.

Billy Barbour

Barbour's departure for Accrington in 1888 was universally unpopular with Queen of the South Wanderers fans, who wanted him to stay. The Scottish club had been suspended for professionalism, Barbour being one of those found to receive free groceries in lieu of pay.

Goal Nets

Goal nets were another invention that were introduced to resolve 'we wuz robbed' disputes, the aim being to determine whether the ball had gone between the posts. The impetus for nets came with the introduction of the Football League. The first season saw a number of disputes over whether the ball had or hadn't gone into the goal.

On 29 September 1888, Burnley players protested strongly at the awarding of a last-minute winning goal by West Brom's Charlie Shaw on the grounds that 'keeper Robert Kay had gone over the bar when he fisted away the forward's shot. In October 1888, Burnley players also felt that Wolves' opening goal in a 4-0 win had gone over the bar.

Then on 15 December, Blackburn Rovers were 2-0 down at home to Notts County. It was a foggy day and Rovers were desperate to hang on to their unbeaten home record and got back into the match just after the hour when 'they scored the first goal – or rather it should say were allowed the first goal, for the ball went fully 2 feet over the bar, but owing to the mist Mr Norris could not see it and forward Jimmy Brown claimed vociferously', reported the *Blackburn Times*.

Back in the game at 1-2, Rovers stormed on to win 5-2 and County's players were not pleased. A month later in January 1889, West Brom had to be persuaded not to leave the field when, 2-1 down away to Notts County, they were convinced the ball had passed between the posts from a Jem Bayliss shot. Not so, said the referee, Mr McIntyre of Manchester, and with no net to catch the ball there was no way of proving otherwise and the Throstles lost 2-1.

Later in 1889, Everton were playing at home to Accrington before an Anfield crowd of 10,000. The referee was J. J. Bentley, one of the main men behind the founding of the Football League who later became its president. Accrington took an early lead through J. Entwistle but,

> With a goal against them, the home lads played up with more determination and Latta from a position almost parallel with the goal posts kicked the ball splendidly, a great cheer being sent up by the crowd. The referee however ruled that the ball had not gone through and he was promptly and vigorously

hooted ... The decisions of Mr J. J. Bentley at this point roused the fire of the crowd, and there were loud cries of disapprobation, which were certainly not justified.

(The Liverpool Courier)

Watching this match was civil engineer John Brodie who, appreciating the referee's difficulties, set out to resolve them. Even though a year later Everton again suffered when Blackburn Rovers, through Jack Southworth, scored with a shot that most Evertonians were convinced had gone over the bar, a solution was now in the offing. (*See report of match on 29 November 1890.*)

Brodie had taken out a patent for his 'net pocket' and, after resolving a dispute with the FA over royalty fees, these were trialed and then first officially used on Monday 12 January 1891 in the North *v.* South match played at the Forest Ground, Nottingham.

As they were made on Merseyside, it was appropriate that a local player was the first to put the ball into them – Fred Geary scoring after quarter of an hour.

They were generally agreed a success, such that *Cricket and Football Field* reported on 17 January 1891, 'Mr Brodie's goal nets are likely to be generally adopted. They are to be used in the Corinthian – Everton match next Saturday.'

By the start of the 1891/92 season every major team was using them. Yet goal nets are not compulsory and, despite being mentioned as a necessity in all competition rules, a game could theoretically go ahead without them.

Nets may be attached to the goals and the ground behind the goal, provided that they are properly supported and do not interfere with the goalkeeper.

(*Laws of the Game 2008–09 FIFA*)

Brodie Avenue in Liverpool is named in John Brodie's honour, and an English Heritage blue plaque is positioned at the late Victorian detached villa he occupied in suburban Ullet Road. He died in 1934, aged seventy-six.

Rams Thrashed

League Game 5
Saturday 4 October 1890
Everton 7 (Geary 3, Milward 2, Chadwick, Kirkwood) *v.* Derby County 0
Venue: Anfield
Attendance: 12,000

Everton: J. Angus, A. Hannah, D. Doyle, C. Parry, J. Holt, W. Campbell, D. Kirkwood, A. Brady, F. Geary, E. Chadwick, A. Milward.

Derby County: D. Haddow, A. Latham, W. Hopkins, B. Chalmers, W. Roulstone, G. Bakewell, L. Cooper, J. Goodall, A. Goodall, S. Holmes, J. McLachlan.

Despite the dull weather, the Anfield pitch was in good shape when the game got underway at 4.00 p.m. With Latta having been injured in a rough midweek friendly in Glasgow against Third Lanark, the Everton side had a new look, Kirkwood moving to right-wing with Parry coming in at right-half.

The game was less than a minute old when Angus was forced to make a good save after George Bakewell came forward to shoot smartly. This attack was to be one of few Derby mounted during the game, as the east Midlanders were swept away as Everton romped to their fifth consecutive victory.

Milward with a powerful drive started the rout before turning goalmaker, his pass splitting the Derby defence for Geary to double the home side's advantage. Milward then made it 3-0 when he followed up after David Haddow had spilled the ball. Geary made the score 4-0 with his second of the match on thirty-five minutes before creating the fifth, finished off by Kirkwood on the stroke of half-time.

There was little relief after the interval for Derby, although when Geary dribbled though the Rams defence he found Haddow in fine form. When Derby did press, Holt was in irresistible form and the Anfield crowd wildly cheered one huge clearance.

Everton's sixth goal was a beauty, Kirkwood's faultless centre headed powerfully home by Chadwick. Derby, despite the score, were still showing some real fight; Holmes had an effort rightly disallowed for offside, but when he again pushed the ball past Angus the decision of referee Mr Jope to disallow his effort was argued with vociferously by the Derby forwards. John Goodall in particular was angered by what match reporters felt was a poor decision.

Derby's ire intensified when, just seconds before the game's end, Geary added his third goal and Everton's seventh.

Friendly Matches

The match with Third Lanark was one of a number of friendly matches played by Everton during the season, thus earning the club much needed revenue. The game marked Everton's first-ever visit north of the Border. With Celtic and Sunderland also set to face each other the same day, the game kicked off at 12.30 p.m. to allow local fans time to attend both fixtures.

The game was to end in a 1-1 draw. Geary gave Everton an early lead, but Hannah was the star of the game, while there was wild applause from the Scottish crowd for the Everton forward's smart quick passing. 5,000 spectators watched the match. This was a thousand more than had watched the earlier friendly at Anfield between Everton and Stoke that the home side won 1-0 with a goal from Brady. Everton had also earlier beaten the (Sheffield) Wednesday 5-1, Bootle 3-2 and Chester 11-0, all at Anfield.

Before October was out, Everton also played and won 2-1 at Sheffield United, enjoyed a 4-0 away success at Chester and drew 2-2 with Stoke in another away fixture. In November, Everton were back in the Potteries to beat Port Vale 3-0.

Elsewhere
Bolton 4 Aston Villa 0
PNE 1 Blackburn Rovers 2
WBA 3 Burnley 1
Wolves 3 Accrington 0

John Goodall

The top scorer in the inaugural Football League season of 1888/89 was John Goodall. Goodall, known as 'Johnny All Good', was the Preston side's best player, earning him the honour of being known as the first player to pioneer scientific football.

The son of a corporal in the Royal Scottish Fusiliers, Goodall was born in Westminster, London on 19 June 1863, a quirk of fate giving him the right to play internationally for England. After leaving school, Goodall worked as an iron turner and played football whenever possible. He joined Kilmarnock Burns as a fifteen-year-old. A year later he signed for Kilmarnock Athletic and made his senior debut in 1870.

Four years later, in 1884, he was lured south into England with professionalism just round the corner, and thinly disguised financial arrangements were commonplace. Goodall joined the Bolton side, Great Lever. Playing his first game for the Lancashire club against Derby County, he scored five goals in a 6-0 victory.

In August, Goodall switched his allegiance to Preston North End, where he developed a wonderful partnership with Ross. It was during this season that Goodall, who was as quiet off the pitch as he was brilliant on it, first played for England, scoring on his debut against Wales in 5-1 victory. He was to play fourteen times in all, scoring twelve times including two marvellous efforts when England beat Scotland 4-1 in April 1892 – his dad must have been pleased!

At the end of the 1888/89 season Goodall, who stood 5 feet 9 inches tall and weighed 11 stone and 9 pounds, had scored fifty goals in only fifty-six first-class appearances for Preston. His speed over the ground, clever footwork, willingness to shoot from any distance, and his accuracy in front of goal made him one of the most accurate marksmen the game of football has ever seen.

Not that such success was enough to keep him at Deepdale, as within weeks he signed for Derby County. It appears money was the main reason as, along with his brother Archie, who also signed for Derby at the same time, he was given the tenancy of The Plough pub on London Road.

Although Derby won no major trophies while Goodall was there, the side earned a reputation for being the most entertaining in the League, narrowly missing honours on several occasions. Goodall also acted as a figurehead to the young players and in particular to Steve Bloomer.

In 1898, Goodall became one of the first players to write a book on football. Entitled *Association Football* and costing 1s (5p), it provides a fascinating and unique insight into the game at the time. It was dedicated to Corinthian forward G. O. Smith, who Goodall rated as 'the best centre-forward in my time'.

In the book, Goodall offers advice to players, impressions of the game and hints for positions. He describes football as an art that can only be mastered by practice and enthusiasm. He bemoans the professional player who fails to constantly try and improve his game. Although sturdiness is essential to be a goalkeeper, Goodall knocks any idea that there is an ideal size for a footballer and writes 'it is purely a question of skill in the best class, in which there is less rough play than in the modest spheres of football'.

While pace can be a big help, he points out that in the Invincibles side of 1888/89 there was no player with great pace, and that the Preston side were superior as a result of the perfect placing of players and a willingness to work as a team, allied to 'pluck' in never knowing when they were beaten. Having the best eleven players does not always win the match, and while getting excited beforehand was only natural, once a player entered the field it was best if he was cool and could keep his wits about him.

Goodall was also a big believer in players ensuring they had lots of rest between games and making sure of not overeating before a match, believing that no player should eat much in the three hours leading up to one.

Goodall also urged players not to heed advice from the spectators: 'It is a fact that the people can often see openings that the players cannot; nevertheless, the player does best when he follows his own dictates.' Goodall also reminded young footballers that the 'first and last five minutes of a game are just as important as any other', and cautioned against a player losing his temper or becoming frustrated at losing the ball to a good tackle. Goodall was a big fan of Preston 'keeper James Trainer, but also admired the West Brom 'keeper Joe Reader for his accurate kicking to his forwards. Well over a century since Goodall wrote his book, it would still prove an interesting read for any young person seeking to know more about how to play football. Sadly, the book is no longer in print.

First Draw Earned with Late Equaliser

League Game 6
Saturday 11 October 1890
Aston Villa 2 (Paton, Cowan) *v.* Everton 2 (Geary, Kirkwood)
Venue: Wellington Road
Attendance: 5,000

Aston Villa: J. Warner, G. Cox, W. Evans, T. Clarkson, H. Devey, J. Cowan, A. Brown, W. Dickson, J. Paton, D. Hodgetts, L. Campbell.

Everton: J. Angus, A. Hannah, D. Doyle, C. Parry, J. Holt, W. Campbell, D. Kirkwood, A. Brady, F. Geary, E. Chadwick, A. Milward.

Referee: Mr Widdowson of Nottingham

With Everton intent on continuing their fine run, Brady almost opened the scoring on five minutes, but his shot flew just over with Jimmy Warner beaten. There was little, however, that the Villa 'keeper could do ten minutes later when Geary, receiving a Chadwick pass, curled the ball round him and into the goal to give the League leaders a well-deserved lead.

Both Geary and Brady could possibly have made it 2-0 as Everton maintained their pressure, before Chadwick missed when well placed. It was to prove a costly miss, as having hardly been in the game the home side then equalised when Angus was unable to hold off Jim Paton's shot, with the ball just passing over the goal line to make it 1-1 on thirty minutes. The 'keeper did better when he fisted out a Dennis Hodgetts shot as Villa looked to build on their good fortune. With neither side able to assert their superiority, the score at half-time remained level.

It took less than a minute for the home side to take the lead, when after Doyle had fouled Hodgetts in the penalty area (*see p. 45*) Jimmy Cowan beat Angus with the resulting free-kick. Were Everton set for their first League defeat of the season? Geary thought he had equalised, the goal being disallowed for reasons that the match reporters were unable to ascertain, before Chadwick beat Warner only to see his powerful shot rebound back off the crossbar.

Brave 'Keeping

Then, with Geary through, Warner dived bravely down at his feet to grab the ball, the Villa 'keeper performing an act few other custodians would have entertained at the time.

Despite Everton's search for an equaliser, it was Villa who looked the more likely to score again. Albert Brown seemed certain to increase Villa's advantage as the game seemed to be slipping away from Everton, but Parry made a great block to prevent Everton falling further into arrears. It was Hannah, though, who did most to keep his side in the game, making some fine tackles on nearly all the Villa forwards.

The defender was rewarded when Everton stole an equaliser on eighty-seven minutes and if the *Liverpool Courier* and *Cricket and Football Field* are to be believed, the goal was scored by Kirkwood and not, as has been recorded in the Everton history books, Geary.

> There seemed to be no chance of the visitors making a draw, but three minutes from the finish Milward dribbled down and passed to Kirkwood who shot in and performed the feat. Warner dropped on the ball behind the line, and Geary ran up and kicked in order to place the matter beyond doubt, but the ball rebounded from the goalkeeper over the bar. The home team, of course, claimed no goal, but the referee paid no heed to it.
>
> (*Liverpool Courier*)

> Kirkwood, following up made it 2-2.
>
> (*Cricket and Football Field*)

The match had not been a great one, but Everton had maintained their unbeaten start to the season, and by doing so, had demonstrated they had the mental strength to keep playing to the end of the game; a quality that would be necessary if they were to win the title for the first time.

Playing away from home tests the mental qualities of any footballer as they have few friends among the spectators, many of whom are anxious that they should fail. The Villa crowd were passionate – in the first season of League football it was even said they had booed Everton on to the pitch before kick-off – and not averse to jeering their side's opponents. Everton had stood up to a severe test and now had two homes games to follow from which to maintain their lead at the top of the table.

Wellington Road

Villa moved from their first pitch in Aston Park to Wellington Road in Perry Barr two years after their formation in 1874. Shifting a haystack from the middle of the pitch was necessary before any match kicked off, and with a hump near one end and a line of trees down one touchline, facilities were not ideal – especially as Birmingham's first steam tram depot and bus garage was just yards away! The ground was to host two FA Cup semi-finals in 1890 and in 1896, when 35,000 packed it out to witness Wolverhampton Wanderers beat Derby County 2-1. One year later, Villa played their final game there before moving to Villa Park.

In 1888, Birmingham with a population of 470,000 was easily big enough to accommodate a Football League side. The 'city of a thousand trades' had numerous workshops and factories. From one of these, toolmaker's Joseph Hudson's, came the referee's whistle. This replaced the original handkerchief used to indicate the man in charge wished to signal a decision. It is believed that the whistle was first used in a match between Nottingham Forest and Sheffield Norfolk. Hudson's is today still active in the form of Acme Whistles and estimates to have manufactured over 160 million.

Penalty Kicks

Penalty kicks were introduced to prevent teams profiting from deliberate fouls or handballs close to their own goal. When the idea was originally suggested, it had been rejected as implying that some players were ungentlemanly. This was a view totally at odds with the Victorian idea of an amateur gentleman sportsman. After all, surely no one would stoop so low as to cheat their opponents out of a goal by handling the ball when close to their own goal, or even tripping their opponents!

Wealthy Irishman and keen sportsman William Scrum was a man with some clout, and as a member of the Irish football Association he submitted a proposal to the June 1890 meeting of the International Football Association Board for penalty kicks to be legalised.

The 'Irishman's motion' or 'death penalty' was roundly condemned, but public opinion swung in favour after an indirect free-kick was awarded for a deliberate handball on the goal line in the FA Cup quarter-final between Stoke City and Notts County on 14 February 1891. Stoke, having earlier beaten Preston North End and Aston Villa, had high hopes of a first trophy. With County leading 1-0 in the final minute of the game, their full-back Jack Hendry punched a shot off the line when his 'keeper George Toone was beaten. Stoke were given a free-kick on the goal line, but Toone smothered it easily. County won 1-0 and went on to reach the final.

The rules were quickly changed, and on 2 June 1891 the penalty kick rule was adopted in the Laws of the Game. The first side to score from one was Rotherham Town, Albert Rodgers doing the job on 5 September 1891 in a game at Darlington St Augustine's.

In 1998, Gary Lineker made a BBC documentary on McCrum and the penalty kick.

Dennis Hodgetts

Dennis Hodgetts scored Aston Villa's first goal as they beat West Bromwich Albion to win the 1887 FA Cup final. In 1892, when the two sides met again in the final, Hodgetts collected a runner's up medal, but gained his revenge when the Midland sides clashed for a third time at the 1895 final when Villa won 1-0. He made six appearances for England. A remarkably clever player, Hodgetts was unselfish with the ball and always gave everything to the cause.

James Warner

Keeper James Warner was supple, shrewd and agile enough to punch away the hardest of shots at goal. Warner played in two FA Cup finals for Villa, both against WBA, gaining a winner's medal in 1887 and a loser's in 1892. Rumours abounded that he sold the latter game, in which he made the last of 101 appearances for Villa, and irate fans took revenge by wrecking his pub.

Elsewhere
Burnley 1 Bolton 2
Blackburn 3 Sunderland 2
Wolves 5 Derby County 1
Notts County 3 WBA 2
Accrington 1 PNE 3

Two Hard-Earned Points

League Game 7
Saturday 18 October 1890
Everton 2 (Brady 2) *v.* Bolton Wanderers 0
Venue: Anfield
Attendance: 12,000

Everton: J. Angus, A. Hannah, D. Doyle, C. Parry, J. Holt, D. Kirkwood, P. Gordon, A. Brady, F. Geary, E. Chadwick, A. Milward.

Bolton Wanderers; J. Sutcliffe, J. Somerville, D. Jones, A. Paton, J. Davenport, R. Roberts, R. Jarrett, J. Brogan, A. Barbour, J. McNee, J. Munro.

Referee – Sam Ormerod.

Bolton Wanderers arrived at Anfield in fifth place in Division One. They were determined to improve on their showing earlier in the season, and in a sense they succeeded, but not enough to upset the bookmaker's odds that prior to kick off had Everton at 2/1 on to win.

Betting on football matches appears to have arrived with the advent of the FA Cup, first played for in 1871/72, as the first reference to betting on the outcome of football matches appears to be that Royal Engineers were installed as 4/7 favourites to win the first FA Cup final in 1872 – they lost.

Within five years, betting on several matches taking place on the same day appears to have already been established. Not everyone was happy with this state of affairs, with the *Birmingham Guardian* declaring it was a 'nuisance' as it had led many men to bet their week's wages on the outcome of the 1887 final between Aston Villa and WBA, and for years the football authorities maintained a strict policy of non-engagement with bookmakers and the gambling industry.

Much later in 1936, the Football League even went as far as issuing fixtures only a couple of weeks in advance to prevent pools promoters preparing coupons in time for distribution. This laughable effort lasted all of two weeks with a result of League 0, Pools 1.

However, in January 1948, Pools Betting Duty was introduced at 10 per cent and raised to 20 per cent in October as the government looked to cash in on the increasing popularity of the Treble Chance, which in 1950 saw Mrs E. Knowlson of Manchester become the first to scoop £100,000. Seven years later, Mrs Nellie McGrail of nearby Stockport won £200,000, becoming the first to receive a cheque from a well-known celebrity, comedian Norman Wisdom in this case.

Alex Barbour kicked off the game at 3.35 p.m. before 12,000 spectators. They had to wait sometime before Brogan fired the first real shot on goal, Angus making a fine save.

However, it was John Sutcliffe, Angus's counterpart in the Bolton goal who provided the first real talking point, when he pulled down the crossbar such that Geary's shot which seemed set to make it 1-0 passed over rather than into the goal. With the bar soon restored, the game became a fierce no-holds-barred battle, and Holt upset a number of the away side by a series of rough challenges.

Bob Roberts was not too far away with a long-range shot, but teammate James Brogan should have done better with an effort from a much closer range. Just before half-time, Brady saw his effort superbly saved by Sutcliffe to keep the score goalless at the interval.

Everton started the second period by pushing forward and Sutcliffe was forced to save a Milward drive as Everton sought to grab the first goal. Kenny Davenport, who the *Liverpool Courier* reported 'stuck to him like a leech and was applauded for concluding a clever piece of play successfully', was heavily marking Milward. The defender's efforts looked like they had been rewarded when Bolton created a great chance, but Jimmy Munro fluffed a shot from less than a dozen yards. There was then a heavy dispute when it appeared that Angus had punched Brogan's shot away from behind the line. However, the referee ruled against the visitors.

With time running out, Milward and Chadwick combined down the Everton left and the latter seemed to have opened the scoring with a vicious drive, only to see Sutcliffe make a splendid diving save.

With five minutes to play, the deadlock was though finally broken when Gordon, making his Everton debut, worked his way round Roberts before cutting the ball back to Brady, whose shot was too powerful for Sutcliffe, to the obvious delight of a relieved Everton crowd.

Two minutes later the contest was decided when, after combining with Gordon, Brady superbly dropped his shot over Sutcliffe giving Everton a 2-0 win and maintaining their position at the top of the table. It had been a hard fought contest, in which Everton's determination to keep fighting to the final whistle had won out at the end.

Kenny Davenport
Scorer of the First League Goal

Kenny Davenport played for Bolton Wanderers for eleven seasons, joining the club from Gilnow Rangers 1883. He was born in the Deane area of the town, a stone's throw away from Pikes Lane. By the time League football commenced in 1888/89, Davenport was already an England international, the first in Bolton's long history. He played once more, scoring twice in a 9-1 victory against Ireland in Belfast in 1890.

Normally an inside-left, Davenport made fifty-six League and twenty-one FA Cup appearances for Wanderers, scoring thirty-six goals. Davenport was the scorer of the first-ever League goal at 3.47 p.m. on Saturday 8 September 1888.

On the opening day of the season five matches were played:

Bolton Wanderers – Derby County
Preston North End – Burnley
Wolves – Aston Villa
Stoke – WBA
Everton – Accrington

For many years since, it has generally been accepted that Aston Villa full-back Gershom Cox scored the first League goal when he put through his own goal after thirty minutes of the match at Wolves' Dudley Road ground. This appears to have been based on the belief that, unlike the other games that were advertised to start at 3.30 p.m., the Wolves *v.* Villa game kicked off at 3.00 p.m. This is what a number of respected authors and historians told me when I was working on my book: *The Origins of the Football League: The First Season 1888/89.* Not convinced, and knowing that other matches involving Wolves in the early part of the season commenced at 3.30 p.m., I was keen to discover the truth.

This took some considerable time. Newspapers in Birmingham and the West Midlands were rigorously checked, all to no avail. The newspapers *Athletic News* and *Cricket and Football Field* also proved unfruitful. Fortunately, Robert Boyling, a Millwall fan and a librarian at the Colindale newspaper library, was prepared to help out. In his dinner hours he trawled through every paper before finally finding what was needed; an advert for the kick-off time for the Wolves – Aston Villa game. This is taken from *The Midland Evening News* of 7 September 1888. When this showed 3.30 p.m. it meant that by scoring an own goal on thirty minutes, Cox had scored at 4.00 p.m. on 8 September 1888. There were no goals scored before half-time in the Everton *v.* Accrington and Stoke *v.* WBA games. It meant that if anyone had scored before Cox, it had to be in the other two matches.

For this we are indebted to the reporters of the *Cricket and Football Field*, who reported on the kick-off times at Pikes Lane, Bolton and Deepdale. As a result, we know the match at Bolton kicked off 3.45 p.m. and that at Preston at 3.50 p.m.

This is what happened at the Bolton match that was played at the Wanderers Pikes Lane Ground:

> The visitors were late in making an appearance and some impatience was manifested at the delay. At a quarter to four the County kicked off with the sun at their backs, the Wanderers having won the toss but preferring to give their opponents the advantage ... The visiting right made an attack that was cleared by 'Bethell' but the ball was kept in the Wanderers quarter for a minute or so, until Davenport coming away transferred the play to the other end, and in two minutes from the start Kenny had scored a fine goal for the Wanderers. A protest for offside was raised in vain.

Davenport repeated his feat within a minute and a third goal was added by James (Jimmy) Brogan before the Preston match had even got underway, with Fred Dewhurst scoring early on for Preston.

Elsewhere
Burnley 1 Blackburn Rovers 6
Derby County 5 Aston Villa 4
Sunderland 2 Accrington 0
WBA 1 Notts County 1
PNE 5 Wolves 1

First Defeat
League Game 8
Saturday 25 October 1890
Everton 2 (Holt, Latta) *v.* West Bromwich Albion 3 (Dyer, Nicholls, Burns)
Venue: Anfield
Attendance: 9,200

Everton: J. Angus, W. Campbell, D. Doyle, C. Parry, J. Holt, D. Kirkwood, A. Latta, A. Brady, F. Geary, E. Chadwick, A. Milward.

WBA: J. Reader, J. Horton, S. Powell, E. Horton, C. Perry, F. Dyer, W. Bassett, S. Nicholls, G. Woodhall, T. Pearson, J. Burns.

West Brom were intent on revenge after being so easily beaten on the opening day of the season, but with six wins and a draw from the first seven League games Everton were naturally confident of maintaining their fine start to the season.

Hannah was missing for the first time in the season after having caught a cold while on a trip to Scotland. Doyle seemed particularly affected by the absence of his fellow full-back, playing very poorly in the first half an hour, during which the away side established what proved to be a winning lead.

The return of Latta was met with general approval prior to kick-off, but it was the away side that started the more brightly on a muddy pitch with early efforts from Tom Pearson and Billy Bassett before Milward had the first shot from Everton.

West Brom was in front after just ten minutes, when after Doyle had miskicked to give away a corner, Sammy Nicholls headed home. The same player then rattled the bar as the away side sought to build on their lead, before Everton made a number of attempts on the West Brom goal with Brady, Geary and Latta all firing shots just wide.

However, after Charlie Perry had had a goal disallowed for a foul on Angus, the away team made it 2-0, Pearson hitting a great shot home. If that wasn't bad enough, it was soon 3-0 after Burns hammered Doyle's careless pass past Angus. Although the vast majority of the 9,000 crowd had obviously come hoping to witness another Everton victory, this did not stop them cheering WBA off at half-time as the West Midland side had played extremely well.

In the second period, Everton made a big effort to get something from the game, and a beautiful cross by Milward enabled Latta to touch the ball past Joe Reader to make it 1-3. This was met with loud cheers and inspired confidence amongst the home team, who forced a succession of corners from which Reader was constantly under pressure.

There was a blow when Latta was badly injured, and despite continuing on the field he was unable to play any real effective part in proceedings, giving rise to fears he had returned too quickly from injury and might now been force to take an extended 'rest'. Yet Everton still pressed. Twice Geary hit the post, Reader fisted out a beauty from Chadwick and there was disappointment when Doyle's indirect free-kick sailed past the 'keeper and into the goal without any of the Everton forwards getting a touch.

Holt finally managed to make it 2-3, but try as Everton might they couldn't get a third, with Reader pulling off a number of decent saves to ensure his side took both points home. It had been a disappointing result, but with only one defeat in eight, and with six victories, Everton remained in prime position to capture the First Division championship for the first time.

Reader is a hero, not a flashy star, a cool quiet business like fellow, who can fill the very capable boots of ever such a big man as Bob Roberts.

(*Cricket and Football Field*)

Elsewhere
Accrington 3 Notts County 2
Aston Villa 4 Derby County 0
Blackburn 1 PNE 0
Bolton 2 Sunderland 5
Wolves 3 Burnley 1

Billy Bassett

Regarded as the finest right-winger of his day, Billy Bassett charged down the flank like a whippet before sending over his centre, whether high or low. He was clever on the ball, possessed a powerful right foot shot, and was Albion's joint top-scorer in 1888/89 with eleven League goals. He served the club for a grand total of fifty-one years: thirteen as a player (1886–99), six as a coach (1899–1905), three as a director (1905–08) and twenty-nine as chairman from 1908 until his death in West Bromwich in 1937.

He scored seventy-seven goals in 311 first-class matches, played in the 1888 and 1892 FA Cup winning teams, and in the losing side of 1895. He was capped sixteen times by England, eight coming in successive games, and he was at his very best in the 1893 match when, with Scotland winning 2-1, Bassett played brilliantly to create golden opportunities for Edgar Chadwick and Fred Spiksley to lead England to a 5-2 victory. He also represented the Football League on three occasions, an England XI once and starred in six international trails. From 1930–37 he was a member of the Football League Management Committee, was on the England selection panel in 1936–37 and was also a Justice of the Peace. He was born in West Bromwich in 1869.

Disappointing Display
League Game 9
Saturday 1 November 1890
Notts County 3 (Daft, McGregor, McInnes) *v*. Everton 1 Geary
Venue: Trent Bridge
Attendance: 13,000

Notts County: G. Toone, T. McLean, J. Hendry, A. Osborne, D. Calderhead, A. Shelton, A. McGregor, T. McInnes, J. Oswald, W. Locker, H. Daft.

Everton: J. Angus, A. Hannah, D. Doyle, D. McLean, W. Campbell, C. Parry, J. Elliott, A. Brady, F. Geary, E. Chadwick, A. Milward.

Formed in 1862, Notts County are the oldest professional League club in the world. In 1890, County played their homes games at Trent Bridge County Cricket Ground, not moving to their current ground Meadow Lane until September 1910.

With Latta out injured, and Everton unable to locate his replacement Hope Robertson, there was an unlikely opportunity for Jack Elliott to show his paces with manager Dick Molyneux being forced to wait behind to accompany the debutant on a later train. Hannah, although fit, had now contracted the flu and was again absent from the Everton side, and with Holt out there was a further opportunity for Campbell. Everton were playing a Notts County side lying in fourth place, three points behind the leaders.

The game started with a Geary header beating George Toone, but Tom McLean seemed to come from nowhere to hack clear before Milward struck the crossbar with a powerful drive.

When the 'Lacemen' threatened, Tommy McInnes shot just over. From a corner soon after, Harry Daft, receiving the ball on the corner of the penalty area, hit a shot that dipped over Angus to make it 1-0 to the home side amid a scene of great enthusiasm. It had been a goal of real quality from a very good player.

Everton were indebted to Daft when he pushed another shot just wide; they then went on to equalise from a corner of their own, Geary beating Toone from 10 yards out. The speed of the game was such that both sides must have been grateful to hear the referee's whistle for half-time.

Yet things were even more hectic when play resumed; Milward thought he had scored with a great shot that flashed just wide, Elliott struck the crossbar for the League leaders, Brady narrowly missed and then Jack Oswald shaved the crossbar for the home side.

There was a touch of good fortune with the home side's second when David Calderhead's shot hit the bar and appeared to enter the goal off one of the visiting defenders, although in the record books the goal is credited to Andy McGregor. Today, we have a group who analyse disputed Premier League goals and rule on the outcome, but not so back then. Whoever scored, it was still 2-1 to Notts County, and soon after it became 3-1, when McInnes following a dribbling run finished it off with a magnificent shot that gave Angus no chance and helped move his side up to third place in the League. After a thrilling start to the season, Everton was now coming under serious pressure at the top of the League.

*Notts County were known as the Laceman due to industrial Nottingham's association with the hosiery trade and its stocking machine.

Elsewhere
PNE 1 Accrington 1
Burnley 4 Wolves 2
WBA 0 Aston Villa 3
Sunderland 3 Blackburn 1

Notts County – Trent Bridge Cricket Ground
Older even than the Football Association itself, Notts County was formed in 1862 for 'gentlemen only'. Having hired Trent Bridge on a number of occasions

for important matches, a host for County and Test cricket since 1838, County moved there when Nottingham Forest left for a new ground in Lenton in 1883.

Three years later, the architecture of the ground was to start changing considerably, and within another three years a new pavilion, which even today remains the ground's most distinctive feature, had been constructed to take in the action on the large field that was roped off to prevent spectators entering the field of play. It was the continuing prioritisation of cricket at the start and end of the season, forcing County to play elsewhere, that eventually persuaded County to move to Meadow Lane in 1910 where they have remained since.

In 1888 Nottingham, with over 150,000 residents, many employed in the textile industry, could easily sustain a League club.

It was the captain of Nottingham Forest, Sam Weller Widdowson, who played for the club for twenty years who invented shin-guards (pads) in 1874. Worn over the socks, they restricted mobility, but provided protection in an era when the metal toecap was popular with many players, as it was believed to assist power in kicking the ball.

Daft was to enjoy a distinguished sporting career, playing football five times for England, collecting a winner and loser's FA Cup medal and also playing 200 first-class cricket matches for Nottinghamshire. Daft was also selected as a reserve for the England lacrosse team. Quick, and with a good cross on him, Daft was a constant threat to any defence.

Alf Shelton

Shelton joined County after Notts Rangers folded during the summer of 1888. He went on to make over 200 League and FA Cup appearances including the 1891 and 1894 finals, collecting a runner's-up and winner's medal respectively. Hard-working and difficult to beat, Alf Shelton was considered good enough to be selected six times for England. He turned down the chance of higher wages to play for newly formed Liverpool in 1892, and later served as a County director for ten years till 1910.

Title Slipping Away

League Game 10
Saturday 8 November 1890
Blackburn Rovers 2 (Dewar, Southworth) *v.* Everton 1 (Chadwick)
Venue: Ewood Park
Attendance: 15,000

Blackburn Rovers: J. Gow, H. Garstang, J. Forbes, J. Barton, G. Dewar, J. Forrest, J. Lofthouse, C. Hall, J. Southworth, N. Walton, W. Townley.

Everton: R. Smalley, A. Hannah, D. Doyle, C. Parry, J. Holt, D. McLean, H. Robertson, A. Brady, F. Geary, E. Chadwick, A. Milward.

With two consecutive defeats, Everton were in danger of throwing away their fine start to the season when they made the trip to Ewood Park to face the FA Cup holders. Rovers had thrashed the Wednesday 6-1 at the Kennington Oval at the end of the 1889/90 season, a match, which resulted in the first FA Cup final hat-trick by Billy Townley. Only two players have equalled the outside left's feat since – Notts County's Billy Logan in 1894 and Blackpool's Stan Mortensen in 1953. Eight of the eleven players in the Rovers cup final side were in the team to play Everton, including Townley. Angus had paid the penalty for conceding three goals in the two previous games with Bob Smalley taking over in goal for Everton.

Three special trains conveyed around 2,000 travelling fans from Liverpool, and with all ordinary trains also crowded, at least 3,000 of those present were thought to be following the away side. One person who hadn't travelled on the day, however, was the referee – an oversight by the Football League committee had resulted in none being appointed. A request to the editor of *Cricket and Football Field* to take charge had been politely turned down before Mr Lockett, the League secretary, arrived at the ground to officiate.

Kicking off against the wind, the League leaders started badly and Rovers had early shots that Smalley was pleased to see float by. When Everton, with Hope Robertson making his debut, were able to get forward, McLean pushed his shot wide of the post. Hannah blocked a shot from Joe Lofthouse at the expense of a corner, before the home side's pressure brought its rewards when, following a free-kick awarded for a foul by Brady, George Dewar scored. (The ball would have been played to the scorer as the rules, in 1890, did not allow a goal to be scored direct from a free-kick.)

It could have been even worse for Everton, but Townley blazed over from less than a dozen yards. The Everton forwards were largely anonymous, and when they did try to rush forward with the ball John Forbes was quick to block. Holt managed a shot, but John Gow was left untroubled and the away side were grateful for Smalley when he put Nat Walton's shot over the bar.

When Gow was finally forced to save, he made it look easy by being in the right position to gobble up Chadwick's shot from 15 yards. The half ended with Rovers in the ascendancy with Nat Walton firing a shot narrowly wide.

Buoyed by having the wind with them, Everton started the second period in much better shape than they had ended the first. Chadwick hit the post with his second of two quick corners, before Gow saved a long shot from Hannah. A tussle between the players ended with Geary's shirt torn, and changing it in the heavy falling rain can't have been too pleasant. Doyle shaved the bar for Everton before Jack Southworth scored the Rovers second goal, the ball going clean through Smalley's legs to the cheers of the home fans. Everton seemed sunk, but fortunately Walton missed a glorious chance to add to their woes by failing to control a pass from Lofthouse with only Smalley to beat.

Off the Top

Just when it appeared that Blackburn were going to see out the game without any trouble, Chadwick dodged Forbes and easily beat the 'keeper who appeared to totally miss the ball, the gloomy conditions no doubt making both Gow and Smalley's tasks difficult ones. Try as Everton might after this unexpected bonus, they could not manage to get the ball past Gow again and, with Wolverhampton winning 1-0 at Molineux against Bolton Wanderers, the First Division had new League leaders.

Unless Everton got back quickly to their winning ways, they could kiss goodbye to a first League title and it was a demoralised side that left the pitch at the end.

Elsewhere
Accrington 4 Derby 0
Aston Villa 4 Burnley 4
Sunderland 1 WBA 1
Wolves 1 Bolton 0
PNE 0 Notts County 0

William Townley

William Townley was a native of Blackburn and played for Blackburn Olympic before joining Rovers. After starting at centre-forward, he was moved to left-wing, where he soon blossomed and formed a fine partnership with Nat Walton. He was capped twice by England and won three FA Cup winner's medals. A speedy, tricky winger, he could cross the ball with deadly accuracy. He made 124 League and cup appearances for Blackburn Rovers, of which his best was undoubtedly the 1890 FA Cup final. He later became a highly successful coach including spells in charge at Bayern Munich and with the Dutch National side.

James Forrest

One of Blackburn Rovers' greatest players, who played in five successful FA Cup finals between 1884 and 1891. He also represented England on eleven occasions and was the first professional to play for his country in a major fixture, when he turned out against Scotland in 1886. In this match, he was forced to wear a different, coarser shirt than his amateur teammates. Debuting on 27 January 1883 for Rovers, he was still playing twelve years later, combining a keen attitude with strong positional sense and an ability to find his teammates with a shrewd, accurate pass. He later became a Blackburn Rovers director.

Forrest had played three times before, but this was first occasion when he declared himself a professional. In some books it is argued that his shirt was the result of the Scots objecting, professionalism not being legalised there until 1893.

Ewood Park

Rovers had moved at the start of the 1890/91 season from Leamington Road to Ewood Park, signing a ten-year lease at an initial annual rent of £60. Work was still in progress when Everton played there for the first time, but the large grandstand on the riverside of the ground was fully open, and a map of the time shows some rudimentary grass banks on the other three sides of the ground.

In the 1890/91 season, the FA paid Blackburn the compliment of selecting the new ground for the great international contest of the year, England *v.* Scotland, and then angered local fans by choosing a side that did not contact a single Rovers player. Many Rovers fans boycotted the game in protest. As a result, only 6,000 spectators were at the match, cutting receipts to just £334. The selectors were criticised by *Athletic News,* who felt the exclusion of players such as Southworth and Barton was 'not only an injustice to the men themselves, but an injustice to England'. In the event, the star men, Everton's Edgar Chadwick and Johnny Holt, were both natives of Blackburn.

Two Vital Points
League Game 11
Saturday 15 November 1890
Everton 1 (Robertson) *v.* Sunderland 0
Venue: Anfield
Attendance: 12,000

Everton: J. Angus, A. Hannah, D. Doyle, D. Kirkwood, J. Holt, W. Campbell, F. Geary, A. Brady, H. Robertson, E. Chadwick, A. Milward.
    Sunderland: N. Doig, T. Porteous, J. Oliver, H. Wilson, J. Auld, J. Murray, J. Harvey, J. Millar, J. Campbell, J. Scott, D. Hannah.
    Referee Mr M. P. Betts of London.
    Everton's eleventh game of the season was at home to new boys Sunderland, who had been elected to replace the bottom club at the end of the previous season, Stoke City.
    As a trip to the North East meant an away side occurred additional travelling expenses, the Wearsiders had been forced to promise to pay the difference in rail fares between Sunderland and that of the further distance travelled to any of the other League clubs. Costs of teas, hotels and breakfasts were also added to the new club's costs.
    Report from *The Journal*:

Sunderland had been in special training for their game at Everton and left Newcastle Central Station on Friday afternoon in the peak of condition and as hard as nails. They travelled in a very comfortable saloon provided by the Lancashire & Yorkshire Railway Company and the long journey to Liverpool was completed about 10 p.m. They lodged at the Latham Hotel in Houghton St where they had a meal before retiring to bed. Rain fell heavily overnight and on the morning of the match but by kick off time the sun was shining brightly and it was warm.

During the morning, the Sunderland team visited the magnificent art collection at the Walker Gallery, the Docks and the landing stages, as well as other interesting sights in the city. After a light lunch, the team headed for Anfield Road by brake to prepare for the match. Everton made their headquarters at the Sandown Hotel and Jack Angus was visited by his former Sunderland teammates and cordial salutations were exchanged. Both teams dressed at the Hotel and walked to the ground – something of an unbecoming arrangement for as great a club as Everton!

The match aroused enormous interest, and the ground was packed with around 20,000 spectators, many of whom had travelled from Wearside that morning on an excursion train. The ground was well grassed and level, but was sticky and soft due to the rain of the previous night. Sunderland was unchanged, but Everton were without Latta and Geary took his place at outside-right, though after about ten minutes play Robertson and Geary changed places. Sunderland won the toss and played with the sun at their back.

Robertson kicked off and a few midfield exchanges Sunderland made the first attack, but Doyle got the ball away. Milward and Chadwick took up the running for Everton, and Doig saved splendidly from Chadwick's hard and accurate shot. Hannah and Scott took play to the other end, where Angus saved a cracker from Hannah as play swung from end to end. Sunderland were playing a fast game and were frequently applauded, but at last Everton relieved the pressure and their forwards swept up the field.

They looked very dangerous, until Porteous got in a fine challenge to concede a corner. Harvie cleared Chadwick's kick and Sunderland moved into Everton territory. Hannah got in a fine run and won a free-kick that was lofted into the Everton goalmouth, where a terrific tussle ensued with the ball eventually going behind for a goal kick. Campbell was working very hard for the visitors, but it was Everton who showed next when Chadwick put in a fine run that was only just checked by Millar.

Geary got possession in the centre and raced away to fire in a shot that produced a brilliant save from Doig, and for the next few minutes the Sunderland goal was put under severe pressure until W. Campbell shot the ball wide. Doig saved again soon afterwards, but Everton continued to press and seemed likely to score at any moment. Chadwick sent in a stinging shot that flashed just over the crossbar, and moments later banged in another fine shot that went only just wide. Sunderland tried to force the pace at the other end and Scott put a shot wide.

Wilson had Sunderland on the attack again, and the Everton defence was severely tested with Campbell, Harvie and Millar doing some grand work in front of the Everton goal. A goal looked a distinct possibility, but Millars shot went wide of the post. Milward went on a dashing run for the home side but Porteous stuck to him all the way, and forced him to run the ball out of play. Geary, who was now playing at centre-forward, took a pass from Robertson to fire in a shot that Doig palmed away for a corner.

The flag kick was cleared, but Hannah got possession and sent in a long dropping shot that Doig fisted out. The ball dropped amongst a crowd of players, and Robertson brought it under control before steering it past Doig to put Everton ahead. The home fans enthusiastically received the goal, but the many Sunderland supporters in the crowd roared encouragement to their favourites to keep their spirits up. The game was very evenly contested at this stage with both goals being visited in turn.

Doig and Angus were given plenty of work to do, with Angus perhaps the busier of the two. He was fast becoming a big favourite with Evertonians for his magnificent saves. Everton led 1-0 at halftime and after Campbell kicked off, Robertson made a sharp run for the home side to no avail. Some fine combined play from the Sunderland front rank took them deep into Everton territory, where Doyle deliberately fouled Campbell. The free-kick brought a corner, which led to another, but Everton eventually cleared their lines.

Everton took up the running, and Geary sent in a strong shot that Doig fisted away. Campbell and Millar had Sunderland moving again, but Hannah halted their progress and when they came again, Millar wasted a good opening by shooting wide. Sunderland forced a corner, but the home full-backs were in grand form and beat them off. Everton paid a brief visit to the Sunderland goal, but Campbell broke away to bring another save from Angus. Campbell then challenged the goalkeeper and was penalised for holding.

The free-kick gave Everton a brief respite, but Sunderland swept back into the attack and Angus made two saves in quick succession before Holt managed to clear his lines. Everton raced away and probed the Sunderland defence for some minutes, but were unable to find a chink in their armour. With time fast running out, Sunderland were making determined efforts to snatch an equaliser, but Doyle and Hannah stood firm and when the final whistle blew a splendidly contested game ended with a win for Everton.

Elsewhere
Aston Villa 3 Accrington 1
Bolton 1 PNE 0

Notts County 1 Blackburn 2
Burnley 6 Derby 1

Ned Doig

The Sunderland 'keeper was signed from Arbroath in September 1890 as Sunderland fought to establish themselves in the League. He went on to establish a record for the number of seasons with one club with fourteen, before being replaced by Sheffield Wednesday's Andrew Wilson.

Doig may have finished playing well over a century ago, but no Sunderland 'keeper who followed him has possibly been better, and he completed his career, after a later spell with Liverpool, with four League champions medals, five Scottish caps and a Second Division champions gong. According to John Goodall, Doig's 'throw was as good, if not better than, an ordinary pass'. Decisive in coming for the ball, able to withstand the roughest of challenges, agile around the box and a good kicker, Doig was a brilliant 'keeper.

Tom Watson

The Sunderland manager was in charge of the club from 1889 to 1896, during which time Sunderland won three League championships. Watson became manager of Liverpool in 1896, and won the League on a further two occasions. Doig and Watson are buried alongside each other in Anfield Cemetery.

Invincibles Show Their Class

League Game 12
Saturday 22 November 1890
Preston North End 2 (Drummond, Gallacher) *v.* Everton 0
Venue: Deepdale
Attendance: 12,000

PNE: J. Trainer, R. Holmes, N. Ross, B. Kelso, W. Hendry, W. Stewart, J. Gordon, J. Dobson, G. Drummond, J. Drummond, H. Gallacher.

Everton: J. Angus, A. Hannah, D. Doyle, W. Campbell, J. Holt, D. Kirkwood, P. Gordon, A. Brady, F. Geary, E. Chadwick, A. Milward.

Everton entered the second half of the League season with the toughest encounter then in football – an away game at Deepdale, against the winners of the first two Football League titles. Preston had pushed Everton into second place at the end of the previous campaign, and although they were lying in fifth place, a victory against their opponents would move them within a point of the League leaders with a game in hand.

The Preston side contained only three of the eleven that had beaten Wolverhampton Wanderers in the 1889 FA Cup final, when the Lancashire Club became the first to complete the League and Cup 'double.' In addition, by remaining unbeaten in the League during the season, Preston set a benchmark that only Arsenal, in 2003/04, has subsequently matched.

The following match report is taken from *Cricket and Football Field*:

The meeting of these two great teams at Deepdale today had created intense excitement in the football world. The home club had extended their uncovered stand, so that now there are uncovered stands on three sides of the ground and a covered stand on the other. Before two o'clock, a very large contingent of Everton supporters were landed at the adjoining Deepdale station, and by the time the game started, though the weather was unpropitious, there was an attendance of fully 12,000. The ground was in a heavy condition, and a steady breeze prevailed across it.

Punctual to time the teams appeared, the visitors getting a most enthusiastic reception from their 4,000 supporters present. It was noticeable that Jimmy Trainer and Nick Ross were especially patronised on the North End side. Everton kicked off uphill at fourteen minutes to three. The home left were the first to show up, and for a minute Hannah and Doyle had a very anxious time of it. Milward and Chadwick relieved, and the former sent a splendid fast shot just outside the home upright.

Once in their opponents' quarters, the Everton men forced the pace tremendously – they were like cats on the ball, and the home backs had their work cut out. Geary shot over the bar, and the Everton Gordon sent in a hot one that Holmes put out of danger. It was now the North End turn. The right-wing and the halves put in some splendid work. Kelso put in a grand long shot and, after the ball had been dodging about for some time, both Hannah and Angus had to save attempts from Bob Kelso and Jack Gordon.

After a free-kick on the home left, Kelso got the ball and sent in a magnificent shot, which Angus only stopped by pulling down the crossbar. Angus had next to clear a low shot from George Drummond. It may be judged that the home team had by this time got into their stride, and they were doing the entire pressing.

Angus saved a good one from Gordon and a free-kick for hands gave the visitors a breathing space. A most exciting episode followed. Gordon and Sammy Dobson had charged Doyle, and the former sent in a hot shot, which Angus cleared as Georgie Drummond charged him.

Everton Backs Overpowered

Jack Drummond shot in, and Hugh Gallacher charged Angus as he cleared, a tremendous scrimmage following, during which Angus and the backs were charged through and a goal registered for North End amid tremendous enthusiasm. This was after sixteen minutes of play. From the restart, Milward got up the left side and shot high over the North End bar.

The Everton forwards made a most persistent attack, Brady finally kicking wide.

Then the North End right forced a corner from Doyle, but the defence continued fine, though Gallacher, from a pass by Sammy Dobson, made Angus save a hot one. The pace was by this time slowing down, the heavy ground telling on both sides. From a grand run by Drummond, Dobson put it through, but the point was disallowed on an appeal for offside against the last-named.

North End were having the best of matters, combination being grand, and it was only now and again that Everton could get away. Angus saved a grand shot from J. Drummond and then the visitors retaliated. The Everton forwards made Trainer save against the post, and soon repeated the attempt. A corner to North End was useless. Everton had a free-kick for hands in the home quarters, and had another for a free-kick against Dobson. The home team had then a free-kick, and from a run by the right-wing, Angus had again to clear. Geary was tripped, but the free-kick came to nothing, a free-kick to the home team also being useless.

Both sides were tackling with determination, the home team so far working like Trojans. Everton made Bob Holmes, Nick Ross and Kelso to clear from the front of goal, Brady and the left-wing showing up well, but Geary was too well watched to get away much. A free-kick was given against Campbell for throwing Dobson. Angus saved one from Drummond against the post, and a corner following Drummond shot the second just on the interval.

The second half was played in semi-darkness and both sides were much slower, the ground being very heavy. Both goalkeepers were soon troubled, and Everton showing to more advantage than in the first half.

Trainer had to come and put over the bar, and Geary was just floored as he was about to shoot. The home forwards were occasionally dangerous, and the two Drummonds and Gordon showed to such advantage that Angus had to save more than once.

With twenty minutes to play it was impossible to see the ball across the field. Both sides were making spasmodic runs, and there was some grand defence on both sides. Ross played brilliantly, and Holmes, Doyle, and Hannah never made a mistake. The last few minutes were played in a pelting rain, and the game came very slowly. Many of the spectators left the field before the finish.

Elsewhere
Accrington 4 Sunderland 1
Aston Villa 5 Bolton 0
Blackburn 5 Burnley 2
Derby 3 WBA 1
Notts County 1 Wolves 1

Deepdale

Deepdale had already been used for football three years before North End were formed in 1881, and quickly established themselves as one of football's leading lights with a series of high-profile friendly games against first class Scottish opposition and the likes of Old Carthusians.

By 1883, a large stand holding 600 had been erected on the west side of the ground, and this was followed later by a smaller one with a press box in between. The subsequent success it brought saw the club advance adventurous plans for a new stadium next door, but these were to wait until the start of the twentieth century, by which time bigger, more ambitious rivals had overtaken Preston, both on and off the field.

Deepdale witnessed English football's highest victory, when on 15 October 1887 Preston beat Hyde FC 26-0 in the first round of the FA Cup. Four players scored hat-tricks, including Jimmy Ross, who struck eight times.

With Preston still at Deepdale, the ground is the oldest continuously used site for League football anywhere in the world.

In 1890, the pitch at Deepdale was not particularly conducive to good play, often being heavy in the middle with the ball sticking in the mud on wet days. Nevertheless, Preston still played some fine football on it.

Bob Holmes

A left-back, and the only player to play in every League and FA Cup game in the 1888/89 season, when Preston did the League and Cup 'double'. The Preston-born player also played seven times for his country, including captaining England in the 6-0 defeat of Wales in March 1894. Holmes played a total of 300 League appearances for Preston, scoring just the once in a 1-1 draw against Burnley in October 1895. He served as the president of the Football Players' Union in the mid-1890s as the players sought, unsuccessfully, to increase their wages. He later acted as trainer to Dick, Kerr's Ladies, a team of Preston factory girls who drew large crowds as women's football blossomed from 1917 to 1921.

George Drummond

Just eighteen years old at the time, Drummond scored a hat-trick on his debut against Accrington in September 1883. Had travelled south after learning to play football with St Bernard's and it was his value as a versatile player, able to play in virtually every position, that kept him in the side for so many years that in 1900 he was rewarded with a testimonial match that saw the current side play the 'Old Invincibles'. A crowd of 6,000 turned out.

Fiery Lancashire Encounter

League Game 13
Saturday 29 November 1890
Everton 3 (Geary 2, Brady) *v.* Blackburn Rovers 1 (Southworth)
Venue: Anfield
Attendance: 11,000

Everton: D. Jardine, A. Hannah, D. Doyle, D. Kirkwood, J. Holt, W. Campbell, P. Gordon, A. Brady, F. Geary, E. Chadwick, A. Milward.

Blackburn Rovers: J. Gow, T. Brandon, J. Forbes, J. Barton, G. Dewar, J. Forrest, J. Lofthouse, H. Campbell, J. Southworth, N. Walton, W. Townley.

Having won both their games since beating Everton at Ewood Park at the start of November, Blackburn arrived level on points with the hosts, just one point behind Wolves with a game in hand. Many Rovers fans were convinced that their side could emulate the achievement of Preston North End two seasons earlier by completing the League and FA Cup 'double' at the end of the season. With half the League season behind them this was a vital 'must win' match for both clubs, but especially for Everton, who could not afford to lose their fifth game in six.

With ice on the pitch, officials from both sides and the referee Mr Jope were seen taping the pitch beforehand, and although a game would certainly be played, as a good crowd of spectators had assembled, it took a little while for it to be agreed that the pitch was good enough to declare it a 'League game', which was met with a great cheer from all those present.

Fog, however, never a friend of the football fan, had decided to worm its way across the field and when the game kicked off at 2.37 p.m. it made it difficult for many to see the entire game. This led to the surreal experience where one end of the ground could hear about the excitement at the other, but have no real idea what might be happening. Fortunately, by the time the match had been in progress for the first half an hour the fog had cleared sufficiently for all to witness a very decent game of football.

The away side took an early lead when Jack Southworth, showing the pace for which he had become famous, dodged past the Everton half- and full-backs to hit a shot, which the home side believed had gone over the bar rather than under it. In the absence of goal nets until the start of the following season, this left the referee to decide. On this occasion, he agreed with the view of the Rovers players that it was a goal, and Everton debutant David Jardine had conceded his first goal. The match restarted with Everton in desperate need of a quick reply.

At first it seemed that Blackburn might have the measure of the Everton forward line but on twenty-two minutes an equaliser arrived when following clever play Geary pushed the ball over the goal line to make it 1-1.

Great Tackling

The game was now fiercely contested, and when Billy Townley was challenged by Kirkwood the cheers when the Everton half-back came away with the ball were then stilled when the Rovers man recaptured the ball, only for Hannah, to wild applause, to once again rescue the ball for Everton. The players on both sides were aware of just how important a victory would be, and as they battled for the ball the crowd at Anfield was captivated.

When a corner from Rovers was cleared, a ball back over the Everton defence was punched away by Jardine from 25 yards out. Today it would be a 'straight red' and an early bath, but not in 1890, as not until 1912/13 were rules introduced to restrict the 'keeper's handling of the ball to the goalmouth area only.

On twenty-nine minutes, Everton grabbed the lead, when as John Gow grabbed the ball he was shoulder-charged, ball and all, into the net by Brady for what would today be a clear foul and a booking for the forward. Not so in the 1890s, and Everton had taken the lead. On forty-four minutes, Everton struck again, Geary, despite appeals for hands, scoring his second to make it 3-1 at half-time.

If the game had been played in fine spirit, it didn't stop Rovers mounting a half-time protest about the fog, claiming it had affected their performance, the referee refusing to listen to their complaints, and after the then five minute break in proceedings the match restarted.

Geary was fortunate not to receive a nasty injury when he was hacked over by George Dewar. Chadwick hit a long shot over the crossbar as Everton continued to dominate the attacking play, but the entertainment then came in the form of an improvised boxing match as Doyle and Joe Lofthouse got to grips with each other before Tom Brandon and Doyle were sent to change their boots after the referee examined them and found both had studs greater than the regulations allowed.

By the time the match ended it was extremely dark, especially for the Blackburn Rovers side beaten 3-1, a result that maintained Everton in second place in the table, just a point behind Wolverhampton Wanderers with nine games of the League season remaining. It meant that the following weekend's game at Molineux would go a long way to deciding who might capture the title.

Jack Southworth

1890/91 League top scorer with Blackburn.
1893/94 League top scorer with Everton.

Southworth was Blackburn's first truly prolific goalscorer. Born in the town in 1866, he initially turned down Rovers request to join them and remained with local rivals, Blackburn Olympic, the 1883 FA Cup winners.

Above: A drawing of Anfield. (Reproduced with the permission of Tony Onslow)

Below: Daniel Doyle's grave.

Above left: Dan Doyle, who played brilliantly for Everton in the 1890/91 season.

Above right: McGregor statue outside Villa Park.

Below: An advert for football boots.

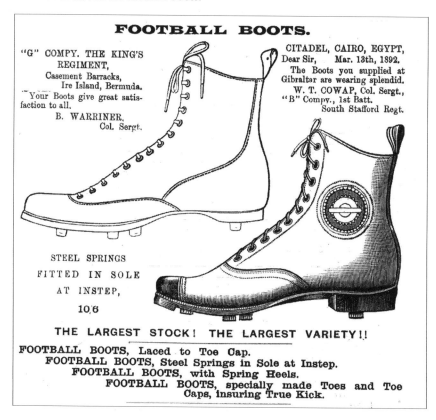

FOOTBALL BOOTS.

"G" COMPY. THE KING'S
REGIMENT,
Casement Barracks,
Ire Island, Bermuda.
Your Boots give great satis-
faction to all.
B. WARRINER,
Col. Sergt.

CITADEL, CAIRO, EGYPT,
Dear Sir,   Mar. 13th, 1892.
The Boots you supplied at
Gibraltar are wearing splendid.
W. T. COWAP, Col. Sergt.,
"B" Compy., 1st Batt.
South Stafford Regt.

STEEL SPRINGS
FITTED IN SOLE
AT INSTEP,
10,6

THE LARGEST STOCK! THE LARGEST VARIETY!!

FOOTBALL BOOTS, Laced to Toe Cap.
FOOTBALL BOOTS, Steel Springs in Sole at Instep.
FOOTBALL BOOTS, with Spring Heels.
FOOTBALL BOOTS, specially made Toes and Toe
Caps, insuring True Kick.

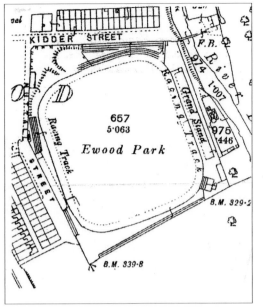

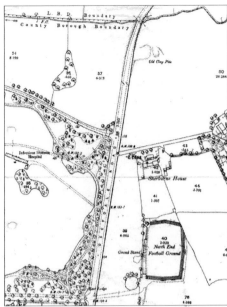

Above left: Map of Ewood Park, Blackburn.

Above right: Map of Deepdale.

Below: Map of Anfield.

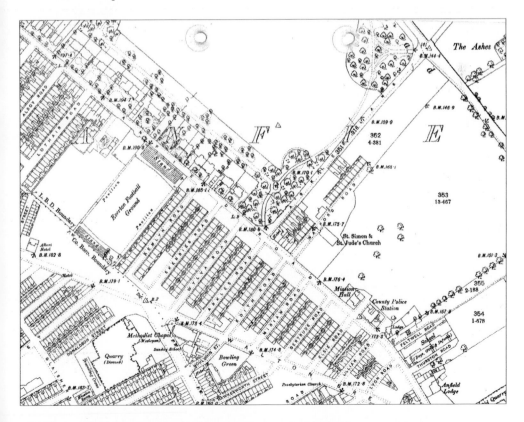

Everton advertised widely for players.

Stoney Lane today.

Above: Pikes Lane today, where the first-ever League goal was scored.

Right: Map of Pikes Lane.

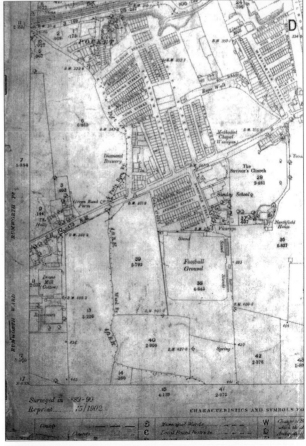

Above: Thorneyholme Road is still a cricket ground today.

Right: Photograph of an English Heritage plaque in honour of John Brodie, inventor of the goal net.

Above left: John Goodall of Preston and England, the best player of his generation.

Above right: Dennis Hodgetts of Aston Villa and England.

Below: Everton *v.* West Bromwich Albion at Liverpool.

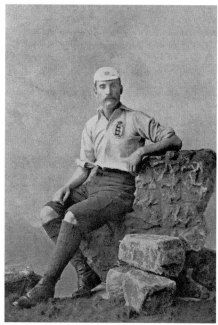

Above left: Billy Bassett of WBA and England.

Above right: Harry Daft of Notts County and England.

Below left: Alf Milward of Everton and England.

Below right: Bob Holmes of Preston North End and England.

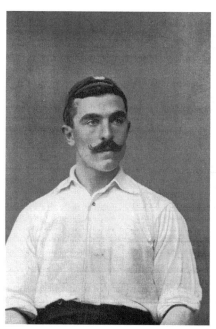

Above right: Trent Bridge in 1891.

Right: The 1891 FA Cup final saw Blackburn Rovers thrash Sheffield Wednesday 6-1, with William Townley becoming the first man to notch a hat-trick in the final.

Below left: John Sutcliffe of Bolton Wanderers and England.

Below right: Ned Doig of Sunderland and Liverpool, who is buried in the Anfield Cemetery.

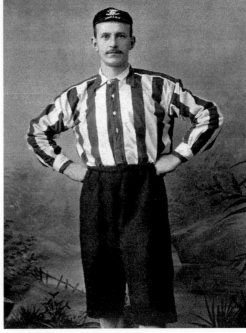

Above: A Lancashire & Yorkshire Railway advert for travel to match, Everton *v.* Blackburn Rovers, 29 November 1890.

Below: A drawing of one of Geary's goals in the match *v*. Blackburn Rovers.

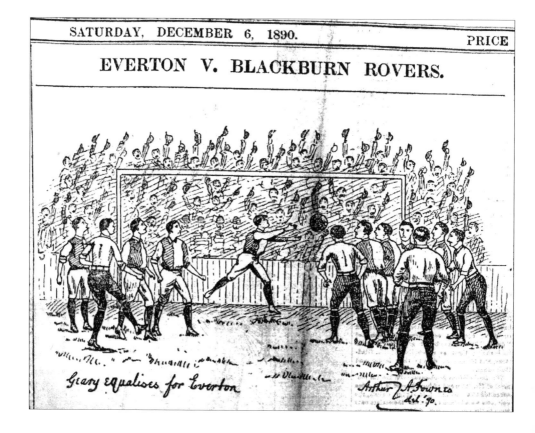

Above: John Southworth of
Blackburn Rovers and England,
who twice finished as top scorer in
Division One.

Right: Map of Racecourse Ground
in 1890.

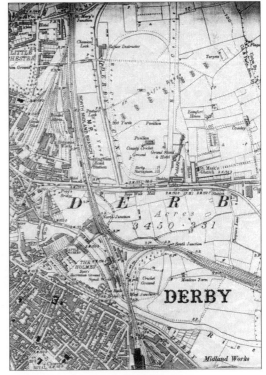

Above: The Racecourse Ground today.

Below left: Johnny Campbell of Sunderland, who finished top scorer in Division One on three occasions.

Below right: James Trainer of Preston North End and Wales.

When he then suffered a serious career-threatening knee injury while playing as a guest for Accrington, it appeared that his football career was over. Switching his attentions to playing between the posts, Southworth showed his all round sporting instincts by becoming Olympic's first-team goalkeeper and helping his side to win the Lancashire Cup final against Rovers in 1885.

In 1886 he then left football for a time, and as he was a keen musician joined a theatre in Chester. Returning home he began playing again at centre-forward for the Olympic, before at the start of the 1887/88 season finally succumbing to the Rovers' charms and signing for them.

He made his debut for the Rovers, ironically against Olympic on 5 November 1887 in an FA Cup tie. As the Rovers then began their new Football League adventure, he captained the side and became a prolific goalscorer. He scored twenty-two goals in twenty-two League appearances in 1888/89, and five goals in five FA Cup ties as the Rovers won the FA Cup in 1889/90 and finished third in the League.

His best season with Rovers was the 1890/91 season, when he was the League's top scorer with twenty-six goals from just eighteen appearances, missing the final four games as Rovers rested players prior to the cup final against Notts County. Nearly half his goals came from four hat-tricks, starting on the opening day of the season in a remarkable game that Rovers lost 8-5 at Derby County.

As he was hitting the net regularly, there was no surprise when he was called up for this second England cap on 7 March 1891. The match against Wales was almost a repeat of his debut two seasons earlier, England again winning 4-1 with Southworth scoring in both. He was to make one further international appearance. It came the following season at Hampden Park, where in a thrilling start England raced into a 4-0 lead after twenty minutes. Southworth scored the third.

Southworth had scored in the previous season's cup final. Rovers had won 6-1 against Wednesday. The 1890/91 final was a lot closer, but Rovers retained the cup in a 3-1 success against Notts County, with Southworth hitting his side's second.

Southworth was transferred to Everton for £400 in 1893, where he was to again finish as the top scorer in the League with twenty-seven goals, nineteen at home and eight away. He made a goalscoring Everton debut in a 7-3 defeat away to Derby County. The England international was also amongst the scorers in Everton's next game, but his opening goal one minute in the game at Villa Park proved mere consolation as the away side slumped to a 3-1 defeat.

There was much more to Everton's play the following weekend, when champions Sunderland came to Goodison Park, Everton having moved across Stanley Park from Anfield at the start of the previous season. At 1-1, some fine passing between Alex Latta, John Bell and Edgar Chadwick opened up the

Wearsiders defence to allow Southworth to run the ball beyond Ned Doig and into the net. Buoyed by their success Everton thrilled a huge crowd of 30,000 by going on to win 7-1.

Everton's First Penalty Scorer

Against Darwen in an 8-1 thrashing, Southworth struck twice. He opened the scoring on five minutes, but it was his second that took him into the Everton record books when, just before the end, Orr was penalised and Southworth stepped up to become the club's first-ever scorer from the penalty spot. Two more goals then followed against PNE at Goodison that the home side, despite a well-hit shot from distance for their second, lost 3-2. Southworth now had eight goals in just eight games.

Away to Sheffield United, it took him just fifteen minutes to open the scoring. Everton had started briskly, and it was no surprise when they took the lead through a well-hit shot, and Southworth might have made it two shortly after but his shot crashed back into play from the crossbar. Alf Milward got Everton's second before Southworth got his side's third in a 3-0 win.

The Merseysiders also struck three times when they travelled to play at Ewood Park, Southworth getting one. Everton were 2-1 down when 'Southworth finished off a smart movement by scoring a "neat goal"', reported the *Liverpool Echo*. In the end, Blackburn did just enough to win a fine game 4-3. With Everton lying in ninth place and opponents Wednesday back in thirteenth in a sixteen-team table, there were fewer than 10,000 in the Goodison crowd for the match played on 23 December 1893.

The away side started in fine form and Fred Spiksley gave them the lead. Southworth then equalised almost immediately, and by half-time he'd added two more and Everton ran off leading 4-1. He was to score his fourth in the second in a game that finished 8-1 in favour of the home side.

Six Goals in a Game

There were 5,000 more for the following weekend's match with WBA, and they witnessed one of the greatest displays ever by an Everton player. Bell gave the home side an early lead, before the Baggies' 'keeper Joe Reader did well to keep out a Southworth effort. The Everton centre-forward was not to be denied for long, and when Latta crossed he headed powerfully home. When Reader could only push out Bell's effort, Southworth was on to the loose ball to make it 3-0, before grabbing his hat-trick shortly afterwards.

Just after half-time, Bell again turned provider to set up Southworth for his fourth and Everton's fifth of the match. WBA was still battling though and reduced the arrears through Owen Williams, only to find Southworth in an unforgiving mood as he rattled home his fifth and sixth in quick succession to make it 7-1. He was the first, and to date only, Everton man to hit six in a single match. Incredibly, it might even have been seven, as just before the end he hit a shot that hit Latta on the way into the net, the effort being disallowed for offside.

Two days later, the record scorer was again doing what he knew best – scoring. It was, however, only the once, in a 3-3 draw at Darwen and just to prove he was after all human, he then missed a penalty as Newton Heath lost 2-0 at Goodison Park. He did, however, get the second and followed this up by hitting one of Everton's goals in a 4-2 win at Deepdale.

On Easter Monday, he again hit the net when Bolton was beaten 3-2 before a 25,000 holiday crowd. It was his twenty-seventh League goal of the campaign and ensured, despite missing the final two League games of the season that he ended, for the second time in his career, as top scorer in the First Division.

Jack Southworth was well on his way to again, finishing top scorer in the following season. Having hit hat-tricks against Small Heath and Nottingham Forest, he ran out at Ewood Park on 20 October 1894 with eight goals in seven games, all of which Everton had won to race to the top of the League and giving rise to great expectations of a second title success in five years.

Southworth was tightly marked by Anderson, who the *Liverpool Mercury* reported 'stuck to him like a leech', and although he managed to net his ninth goal in eight League matches Everton lost their first match of the season 4-3.

The following weekend the Toffees faced Sunderland, and with the sides tied at the top there was a 25,000 crowd at Goodison Park. At 2-1 down with five minutes remaining, they equalised when Dickie Boyle headed Southworth's free-kick home amid great enthusiasm. The Everton centre-forward had again been tightly marked, this time by McCreadie. Sadly, it was to prove his final game. Injured, he never recovered and the loss of such a fine footballer also crippled Everton's League chances. Seventeen out of twenty points had been gathered in the first third of the season and thirty-five goals had been scored. Twenty games later, Everton had scored another forty-seven and taken twenty-five points. Sunderland had done better and finished five points clear of the Toffees.

When his football career ended he turned to his other passion, music, and became a professional violinist. He appeared with the Halle Orchestra, the BBC Northern Orchestra and the Liverpool Philharmonic. His musical skills were such that he played the trombone, euphonium, tuba and violin. His brother James also played for the Rovers at the same time and John, who had a reputation for speed, always maintained his brother was the faster.

During the First World War, he played for Falkirk in Scotland but returned to appear for the Blackburn Rovers once more in 1916. He died in Wavertree, Liverpool on 16 October 1956.

Elsewhere
Notts County 7 Aston Villa 1
Burnley 2 Accrington 0

WBA 3 Derby 4
Wolves 2 PNE 0

Pitch Invasion as Top Spot Recaptured

League Game 14
Saturday 6 December 1890
Wolverhampton Wanderers 0 *v.* Everton 1 (Geary)
Venue: Molineux
Attendance: 6,500

Wolverhampton Wanderers: W. Rose, R. Baugh, C. Mason, A. Fletcher, H. Allen, J. Brodie, D. Wykes, A. Worrall, S. Thomson, H. Wood, C. Booth.

Everton: D. Jardine, A. Hannah, D. McLean, D. Kirkwood, J. Holt, C. Parry, T. Wylie, A. Brady, F. Geary, E. Chadwick, A. Milward.

> At Wolverhampton, in dull, but good football weather. The ground was in excellent condition, and a gate of 8,000 lined the ropes. The game was exciting, and caused immense interest.
>
> (*Cricket and Football Field*, 6 December 1890)

Everton kicked off, and within the first few minutes thought they had taken the lead when Milward forced the ball home, only for the goal to be ruled out for offside. Rose then made a fine save from Chadwick, whose fine dribbling run had given him a shooting opportunity.

A heavy foul on Geary by Albert Fletcher left the Everton centre-forward requiring attention, and it was becoming clear that the home side had earmarked Geary as the man to keep a tight grip on. Wolves was unlucky not to take the lead when Harry Allen's free-kick bounced off the unsighted Jardine and was hacked clear by McLean.

Everton's initial grip on the game was slowly being broken, and in their determination to stay on level terms, the away side committed a number of fouls that incensed the crowd. This intensified when Everton struck what ultimately proved to be the only goal of the game, and although it was Geary who got the final touch much of the credit was Brady's, who after beating John Brodie, provided a wonderful pass that cut out the Wolves defenders and left Geary needing to apply the simplest of touches for Rose to be beaten.

As an inside-forward, Brady was capable of creating a goal out of nothing, and his ability to pass with delicacy had been learned through experience. The art of passing lies in the placing or rolling of the ball so that the player receiving it shall lose no time in proceeding and Wolves had been thrown back on their heels.

Stung by going a goal behind, David Wykes brought a splendid save from Jardine, before Geary's darting run was only ended when Charley Mason dispossessed him with a well-timed tackle. Everton, with Geary prominent, were now providing the Wolve's defence with a severe test. Thomson rallied his men, and when a determined attack was made on the Everton goal the crowd's anger was again roused when Wykes was tripped.

Rough Encounter

At half-time Everton led 1-0, but with nineteen fouls equally divided the game was quickly turning into a rough one. It continued so in the second half, with the game deteriorating into a spectacle. Geary was still nevertheless showing himself to be one of the best players on the field, and Rose saved his shot at the expense of a corner. There then began a period of Wolves pressure, and Charlie Booth, Harry Wood and Thomson could all have done better when well-placed. Wykes was again the subject of a heavy challenge, this time by Kirkwood, and as foul followed foul the crowd became increasingly restless.

This may well have dissipated if the Wolves forwards had managed to take a good number of opportunities during a frantic final fifteen minutes, but when Geary reacted to being bundled over by Allen by kicking the Wolves half-back, a number of spectators could be seen climbing over the ropes around the pitch with the intention of rushing the Everton man.

This is exactly what happened on the referee's final whistle, with the *Cricket and Football Field* reporting the Everton man had been grateful for the assistance of Wolves' Charlie Mason for protecting him from being assaulted before the police arrived to disperse the angry mob, during which at least one spectator was hit heavily with a police baton.

As such, it was some time before the Everton side were able to safely leave the ground, and by the time they arrived by train back in Liverpool news had spread that 'a disgraceful attack had been made' on Geary, and a large crowd was on hand to welcome home the team.

The controversy about whether Geary was right to have defended himself continued, and the verdict depended on which paper you reported for. Liverpudliana in the *Cricket and Football Field* was certain that 'clear instructions had gone out for him to be carefully marked and that it had taken time for Geary to retaliate', which would appear to indicate a degree of sympathy for the Everton man.

In comparison, the *Birmingham Gazette* after reporting that few games have ever had more fouls said the following:

Geary had been badly hurt in the early part of the game but there was no excuse for the petulant attack he made on 'the Wolf' afterwards, and the crack centre had only himself to blame for the demonstration against him at close quarters by the spectators. But for the intervention of the police and the assistance of the other members of the team, Geary would have been roughly handled.

Everton's win had been hard earned; all of the team had played well with Hannah and Geary both magnificent, and the result saw the side move back to the top of the League, well placed to claim a first League title.

Elsewhere
Accrington 2 Derby County 1
Blackburn 5 Aston Villa 1
Burnley 5 WBA 4
Notts County 2 PNE 1

Harry Allen

A formidable defender, who scored thirteen goals in 152 appearances for Wolves between 1886 and 1894. Born in Walsall in 1866, he played for the Town Swifts before joining Wolves. Capped by England on five occasions, he played in two FA Cup finals, scoring the winner (*v.* Everton) in his second of 1893. He was one of only two ever-presents in the Wolves' League side in 1888/89. He retired in 1894 to become a licensee, and died in Walsall in 1895 aged only twenty-nine.

Charlie Mason

Mason was a superb full-back, competent, keen and competitive, who missed only two games out of twenty-two in the first season of League football. Born in Wolverhampton in 1863, he played for Wolves from 1877 (founder member) until 1892, making 108 senior appearances and scoring two goals. He was the first Wolves player to win a full cap – for England *v.* Ireland in 1887 – and later added two more to his tally. In 1888, he guested for West Bromich Albion (the FA Cup winners) in the Championship of the World game against Renton, the Scottish Cup winners. Mason died in Wolverhampton in 1941.

William Crispin Rose

Rose was, in his day, the best goalkeeper in England. Born in London in 1861, he had a varied career that took him from Small Heath (Birmingham) to Swifts (London), PNE (1885/86), Stoke (1886–89), Wolves (1889–94), Loughborough Town and Wolves again (1895/96). He also represented Wiltshire, Staffordshire and London, gained four England caps, and made a total of 155 senior appearances for Wolves, gaining an FA Cup winner's medal in 1893. Instrumental in the formation of the Player's Union (now the PFA), Wood became a licensee and shopkeeper in Birmingham where he died in 1937... 2 miles from Blues' St Andrew's.

Molineux

1890/91 was the second season of League football at Molineux. Wolves moved there after playing at Dudley Road for eight years, but as the team were completing their first season of League football, the Northampton Brewery bought the Molineux sports arena, which included a boating lake and bandstand, as well as an excellent cycling and athletics track surrounding a wonderful field with a playing surface like a bowling green.

With backing from the brewery, Wolves had the developers and gardeners quickly convert the playing area to make it suitable for competitive League and Cup games. Two large dressing rooms were constructed, an office was erected, a grandstand capable of seating around 300 was assembled and along one side of the pitch a shelter capable of accommodating 4,000 spectators was built.

In March 1891, Molineux was to be chosen to stage the England versus Ireland match, one of four full internationals that have been held at the ground.

Wylie the Wizard

League Game 15
Saturday 13 December 1890
Derby County 2 (Goodall, Holmes) Everton 6 (Wylie 4, Brady, Geary)
Venue: Racecourse Ground
Attendance:4,000

Derby County: D. Haddow, J. Baker, A. Ferguson, B. Chalmers, W. Roulstone, G. Bakewell, S. Holmes, J. McLachlan, J. Goodall, A. Goodall, J. McMillan.

Everton: D. Jardine, A. Hannah, D. McLean, D. Kirkwood, J. Holt, W. Campbell, T. Wylie, A. Brady, F. Geary, E. Chadwick, A. Milward.

Despite a heavy overnight frost, the ground was in good condition at the start of the game before a crowd of 4,000. The League leaders were soon in full flow, Chadwick firing just wide within seconds of the start and after just three minutes Wylie, sent scurrying free, finished off a lovely through ball from Geary. Then only John Baker's last ditch tackle on Milward prevented a second, and when Derby did fashion a chance, after McLean handled, McMillan hit his free-kick well wide.

Wylie should have doubled Everton's advantage, but with just the 'keeper to beat he fluffed his shot, before John Goodall showed his ability with a powerful 50-yard run, ended only by a heavy crunching shoulder charge from McLean that today would probably lead to a sending off.

Derby were determined to equalise, but George Bakewell missed from 8 yards when he should have done better. It was a costly miss, and following a great interchange of passes between Geary, Chadwick and Milward, Wylie darted forward to finish off a Chadwick through ball and make it 2-0 to Everton.

David Haddow kept the score down with a lovely save from a Chadwick effort, but on fifteen minutes it was 3-0 when Geary's fine drive left the 'keeper with no chance.

John Goodall brought a good save from Jardine, before the Everton 'keeper showed great ability and courage by diving down at the feet of the onrushing Derby forwards to grab the ball as it flashed across the penalty area.

The Derby 'keeper Haddow then showed his own considerable abilities by denying Wylie, Holt and Geary, and was rewarded when Holmes, denied only seconds earlier by a wonderful save from Jardine, drove home to reduce the arrears. This was the occasion for the ground to be enveloped in a thick mist, and Wylie and Everton's fourth would have been missed by most of the crowd and it was certainly missed by reporters at the game. It nevertheless meant that at half-time Everton led 4-1.

With the fog thickening during the five minute interval, the *Liverpool Courier* reported that Derby's second goal on the restart was 'apparently scored by John Goodall' and, perhaps not unnaturally, the description of the game is a little sparse at this point, although it was possible to see a very heavy Chalmers challenge on Geary that left the Everton man limping badly for sometime afterwards.

Pitch Invaded

Geary had his revenge, though, hammering home Wylie's pass to restore Everton's three-goal advantage, at which point it would appear that some of the crowd, in protest at not getting their money's worth because they couldn't actually see the game, invaded the pitch, and only after the intervention of club officials and the police was it possible to restart the game. Just before the end, Everton again broke away and Brady made it 6-2.

Fog

In the 1904/05 season, Everton were robbed of the First Division title when fog descended on Woolwich Arsenal's ground in Plumstead, South London as the Toffees led 3-1 with just fifteen minutes remaining. When the match was replayed later in the season the Blues lost 2-1, allowing Newcastle United to capture the title for the first time in the Geordies' history.

To make matters worse, after Everton took the lead through Jimmy Settle in the second match, the equaliser came from a player who hadn't been on Arsenal's books when the earlier fixture had been abandoned. Andy Ducat had joined Arsenal in January 1905. He was to later play for England at both football and cricket, and he beat Roose with a fine shot to make it 1-1 at the break. The match seemed certain to end that way when, with five minutes remaining, some lovely passing between the home forwards set up Charlie Satterthwaite, who drove a shot high up into the net.

Everton won their final game of the season, but Newcastle won consecutive away matches at Sheffield Wednesday and Middlesbrough to finish top of the League for the first time. Everton would have to wait until 1914/15 to win the title for a second time.

Elsewhere
Aston Villa 2 Blackburn Rovers 2
Bolton 6 Accrington 0
Burnley 0 Notts County 1
WBA 0 Wolves 1

Racecourse Ground

Cricketing offshoots Derby were formed just four years before the Football League started and played at the Racecourse Ground. This was opened in 1871, and today still remains the home of Derbyshire County Cricket Club. The ground was chosen for the first FA Cup final replay, when in April 1886 the first final ever to be held outside London drew a crowd of 12,000 to witness Blackburn Rovers beat West Bromwich Albion 2-0.

In 1895, disappointment at the continuing failure of the ground's owners, Derby Recreation Company, to prioritise football rather than cricket and horse racing, saw Derby move 1½ miles to the Baseball Ground. This also moved the club closer towards a growing industrial conurbation, at the centre of which was the railway industry, the town of Derby doubling in size from 45,000 in 1851 to over 90,000 in 1888.

Top Beats Bottom

League Game 16
Saturday 20 December 1890
Sunderland 1 (D. Hannah) *v.* Everton 0
Venue: Newcastle Road
Attendance: 12,000

Sunderland: N. Doig, T. Porteous, J. Oliver, H. Wilson, J. Auld, J. Murray, J. Harvey, J. Smith, J. Campbell, J. Scott, D. Hannah.

Everton: D. Jardine, A. Hannah, D. Doyle, D. Kirkwood, J. Holt, W. Campbell, T. Wylie, A. Brady, F. Geary, E. Chadwick, A. Milward.

Referee: Mr Armitt of Leek.

The weather was sharp and bracing with a bright winter sun shining when Everton visited Newcastle Road for this return fixture. The sharp frosts of the past week had made the ground as hard as iron and your heels rattled when you walked on it, but the referee deemed it fit for play. Thus a match, which had created considerable interest in local football circles, was allowed to proceed against an Everton side, who had yet to win on Wearside. Everton had won 1-0 in Liverpool a few weeks previously and the two clubs had been drawn together in the English Cup to add interest to the game.

The crowd soon began to gather, but given the importance of the match the attendance was a little disappointing, with around 12,000 people present. Mr Betts of London had originally been selected as referee, but declined the appointment at the last minute and Mr Armitt of Leek took charge. Everton won the toss and elected to play towards the road end with the sun at their back. Campbell kicked off and Everton raided immediately with Chadwick, Geary and Brady passing their way down, but the final shot was weak and Doig picked up comfortably.

After some midfield exchanges, Scott got a pass from Harvie and rattled in a fine shot that Jardine fumbled, and with Harvie rushing in, Doyle booted the ball clear. Auld got the ball through to Campbell, but A. Hannah robbed him to send Brady dashing away to the other end. Oliver blocked Brady's shot and when the ball rebounded Geary shot wide. Smith had Sunderland back on the attack, but Doyle kicked away. Harvie, Smith and Hannah got away again, but the attack ended when Hannah was caught offside.

The free-kick sent Wylie dashing away, but Murray stopped him. Oliver conceded a corner in Everton's next attack, but Harvie nicely cleared this. Davie Hannah took the ball deep into Everton territory and found Scott, who dropped the ball nicely into the goalmouth where A. Hannah cleared his lines. Wylie got busy for the visitors, but was unable to shake off the attentions of Murray and Everton, who were beaten back to the centre of the field. Milward handled but Porteous's free-kick was poor, and Wylie and Brady got possession and raced past Murray and Oliver.

Auld dashed across to cover, but Geary beat him too and gave Milward a glorious chance to score – but his shot went flying over the bar. Brady put another shot wide of the target and then Everton forced a corner off Oliver, but it came to nothing. Everton continued to press and Sunderland had to defend for several minutes, with Porteous blocking a shot from Brady. Scott handled and Murray had to kick into touch to clear the free-kick. The visitors were hard at work and were playing a splendid game, with Doyle a rock in the Everton defence.

Whenever Sunderland attacked, they were beaten back by his long kicking. A free-kick brought a brief respite for the home side, but Everton were soon attacking again and swarming around the home goal. Sunderland was defending desperately as Everton threatened to score at every turn. A long clearance from Oliver sent Smith racing away, but W. Campbell beat him. Auld dropped the ball back into the visitor's goalmouth where Johnny Campbell had a great chance to open the scoring but missed it.

Doyle checked Sunderland's next attack, but Harvie found an opening to crack in a beauty, only to be given offside. Both sides got free-kicks, but neither came to anything. Sunderland had a spell of pressure and Doyle kicked into touch to clear. W. Campbell put out the throw for a corner, but it went behind. Brady went on a capital run for Everton and cut in towards the home goal, but put his shot wide. A few moments later and Milward did the same when given an opening. A good kick from Murray took play to the other end and when Scott cut the ball back to Murray his shot went just wide.

Play swung quickly to the home end, and Wylie sent in a fierce shot that Doig finger-tipped over the crossbar. The corner was cleared and Sunderland tried to force the play as half-time approached. The attack was only brief, and the visitors rushed away to win yet another corner from which Kirkwood shot over. Half-time arrived soon after to bring to an end a first half in which Everton had enjoyed much the better of the exchanges and was unlucky not to have at least a one-goal lead.

Geary started the second half and Sunderland pressed at once, with Harvie going on a run in which he ran rings round Doyle to bang in a shot that A. Hannah got away. Wilson secured the loose ball but his shot was well wide. A free-kick to Everton sent Wylie and Brady dashing off towards the Sunderland goal, where Oliver's tackle sent the ball into touch. The ball was hurled into the goalmouth from the throw where Doig, believing the ball to have gone out of play, patted it over the goal line. Everton claimed a corner and, to Doig's amazement, the referee agreed.

The corner was cleared, and Geary broke away to send a neat pass to Brady, but when the ball was returned Geary had wandered offside. Some capital work by the home half-backs sent the ball up the home left-wing, where Scott crossed into the goalmouth where Jardine had to rush from his line to beat Hannah to the ball. He threw the ball away, but Harvie secured possession to fire in a shot that went narrowly wide. Sunderland was having more of the play in the second half and Harvie and Smith had them on the attack again.

Smith whipped the ball across and D. Hannah got in a grand shot that flashed past Jardine in the Everton goal to put Sunderland into the lead. Encouraged by their success, Sunderland warmed to their work and applied strong pressure on the Everton goal. Geary made a sudden break and streaked through the home defence to send in a shot that Doig beat away, and when the ball went to Chadwick he put it wide. Sunderland pressed again, and Wilson had a shot that Jardine only just managed to claw away. Scott then sent in a long dropping shot Jardine caught underneath the bar.

He was promptly charged into the net and the ball ran loose. Sunderland claimed a goal, but after long discussions between the referee and the umpires, neither a goal nor a corner was allowed. It was a bizarre decision to say the least. The game became faster and an element of roughness crept in, with several fouls bringing free-kicks. A spell of midfield play followed, and then a foul on D. Hannah brought a free-kick from which Murray drove in a hard shot. Doyle deflected the ball out for a corner and this resulted in a fierce tussle with Harvie, Wilson and Hannah all trying to force the ball home.

Sunderland's pressure was wearing Everton down, and the visitors were struggling to get into the Sunderland half. Just before the close, Smith raced onto a fine pass from Harvie and rattled the crossbar with a good shot. Right on time, Campbell put the ball through to Scott whose low shot scraped the upright and moments later the whistle went amid great enthusiasm from the home supporters.

(*Newcastle Daily Chronicle*)

Elsewhere
Blackburn 2 WBA 1
PNE 6 Derby County 0
Burnley 0 Notts County 1

Photograph Taken
Before the game a photograph of the Everton side was taken and later all the players were given a copy paid for by the Everton committee.

Newcastle Road
This was Sunderland's sixth ground, and was immortalised in the world's oldest and biggest oil painting of a match. Thomas M. M. Hemy's painting of the January 1895 meeting between the Wearsiders and Aston Villa now adorns the main entrance to the Stadium of Light.

Sunderland moved to Newcastle Road in 1886, and quickly built a clubhouse and surrounded the ground with fencing in order to allow for an admittance charge to be made. A grandstand and press gallery were erected, and the ground was good enough to be selected to stage the England game against Wales in March 1891.

Tom Porteous
Porteous became the first Sunderland player to win a cap when he made his only England appearance against Wales in 1891. A good tackler, speedy with good ball control, he was one of the first full-backs to pass his way out of trouble rather than hacking it clear as was the tradition of the day. He won two League champions medals with Sunderland in 1892 and 1893.

Johnny Campbell
Campbell had won the Scottish Cup with Renton before moving south and becoming a prominent member of 'The Team of All the Talents' that

captured the League title in 1891/92, 1892/93 and 1894/95, when Campbell topped the League's scoring list on each occasion. Campbell wracked up 150 goals in 215 appearances for Sunderland, before helping Newcastle win promotion in 1898 and then quitting the game when, by becoming a licensee, he broke the Magpie club rules.

Back to the Top

League Game 17
Friday 26 December 1890
Everton 3 (Milward 2, Chadwick) *v.* Accrington Stanley 2 (Barbour, Whitehead)
Venue: Anfield
Attendance: 14,000

Everton: D. Jardine, A. Hannah, D. Doyle, D. Kirkwood, J. Holt, C. Parry, T. Wylie, A. Brady, F. Geary, E. Chadwick, A. Milward

Accrington: T. Hay, R. McDermid, J. McLennan, M. Sanders, G. Haworth, J. Tattersall, P. Gallocher, J. Whitehead, T. Pendergast, J. Stevenson, A. Barbour.

This fixture took the place of the annual local struggle between the two strongest Liverpool sides, Everton and Bootle. It attracted a good-sized crowd, who saw a very decent match at the end of which Everton had moved a step closer to a first League title.

The home side started the game in fine form, and were soon ahead when McLennan was unable to fully clear a dangerous cross, and in the melee that followed Chadwick shot a splendid goal.

Geary then beat Jack McLennan for pace, but Tom Hay fisted his shot away to keep Accrington in the game. Everton continued to hem Accrington within their own half, and the home side made it 2-0 with a great goal, Milward hitting a curling, dipping shot from 25 yards that Hay never had any chance of stopping.

Great Fight-Back

Yet Accrington seemed by no means dismayed by these early brace of goals, and were soon back in the game when Alex Barbour scored following a corner. Whitehead then shocked the home crowd by equalising, beating Doyle with a lovely shimmy before smashing a great shot past Jardine. The score was 2-2. It was becoming some game for the large crowd.

Wylie had a chance to restore the Everton lead, but it was the away side that should have taken the lead when Bobbie McDermid's long ball left Tom Pendergast and John Stevenson with only Jardine to beat. When they dallied, the 'keeper was out like a flash to kick the ball away to touch. This meant that when the whistle sounded for half-time the game was tied at 2-2.

Barbour was narrowly wide with a long dipping shot as Accrington started the second half in good form. Everton were struggling to assert themselves, although Geary might have done better with a shot from 15 yards in a rare chance for the home side. Pat Gallocher's clever ball gave Whitehead a great chance, but the Accrington man shot wastefully wide. Alex Barbour maintained the pressure, Jardine saving low down.

Accrington was threatening to produce a major shock and Everton were hanging on. Wylie relieved the pressure, and with Accrington tiring as the game moved into the final quarter, Everton finally pushed back the east Lancashire side.

Moment of Magic

Things looked bad, though, when Geary was injured. Forced to move to outside-left, the Everton centre-forward then saw his replacement Milward score a sensational winner. Picking up the ball just inside the Accrington half, Milward surged forward and hammered an unstoppable 20-yard shot past a despairing Hay for what proved to be the winning goal.

There were loud, prolonged cheers at the end. It had been a fine game, three great goals had been scored, and Everton had moved one step nearer a first League title. The Christmas crowd had enjoyed a great Anfield day out.

Patrick Gallocher (or Gallacher)

Pat Gallocher has the distinction of scoring Burnley Football Club's first-ever League goal in the Turfites' 2-5 defeat at Preston on the very first day of League football, 8 September 1888.

Gallocher left his native Scotland in 1883, aged just nineteen, to join Padiham, then one of Lancashire's leading clubs. After occasionally appearing for Burnley as a guest player, Gallocher moved to Turf Moor in the summer of 1886 and was virtually an automatic choice in the Burnley team for the next three years. A very quick and tricky player with wonderful close ball control, Gallocher, nicknamed 'the Artful Dodger', played in all but two of Burnley's League matches during that historic inaugural season of 1888/89.

He joined Accrington in March 1889, scoring on his debut in 'the Owd Reds' last match of the season. He spent two full seasons as a regular at Thorneyholme Road, playing in both defence and attack, before leaving to return to his native Scotland in 1892. Pat Gallocher later joined the Army and served his country with distinction in South Africa during the Boer War.

Elsewhere
Aston Villa 0 Sunderland 0
Derby 1 Bolton 1
Wolves 2 Blackburn 0

Thrilling Entertainment on Icy Pitch

League Game 18
Saturday 27 December 1890
Everton 7 (Chadwick 3, Latta 2, Brady, Milward) *v.* Burnley 3 (McLardle 2, Hill)
Venue: Anfield
Attendance: 8,000

Everton: D. Jardine, A. Hannah, D. Doyle, D. Kirkwood, J. Holt, W. Campbell, A. Latta, A. Brady, F. Geary, E. Chadwick, A. Milward.

Burnley: A. Kaye, A. Lang, J. Walker, W. McFettridge, T. Patterson, J. Keenan, J. Oswald, A. McLardie, Lambie, A. Stewart, J. Hill.

With the weather more agreeable for skating, the likelihood beforehand of a decent game was perhaps remote, but football has a habit of producing the unexpected, and this was one such occasion, with both teams providing thrilling entertainment for the crowd.

When the two teams ran out on a pitch lightly covered by snow, there was huge cheer when it was realised that Latta, missing since late October, was among the home eleven. Within four minutes, the crowd's favourite had given them even more to cheer when, from his second shot, he beat Archie Kaye to put Everton a goal up.

Burnley was level almost from the restart. Alex McLardie, receiving a Hill centre, made space before giving Jardine no chance. It was 1-1 and not even six minutes had gone. There was then a real shock for the home side, when surging forward McLardie drove his side into the lead following a tussle in front of the goal. The score was 1-2, and with the Burnley players ecstatic some in the crowd were unimpressed by their display of joy.

It didn't take Everton too long though to pull themselves level, and again it was Latta, who after Brady had fired just over, took advantage of a free-kick to beat Archie Kaye. With both sides having played so well in difficult conditions, no one could have complained if the scores had remained level at half-time, but with seconds remaining Everton retook the lead when Brady, following a scrimmage in the Burnley box, hit the ball high into the goal.

As the teams left the field, there was then a lovely touch when Everton's Toffee Lady made a beeline for Latta and after a cordial shake of the hands bestowed on him a toothsome package in recognition of his services.

The late goal at the end of the first half seemed to have knocked the stuffing out of Burnley. When the match restarted, Everton pinned the East Lancashire side back around their goal. Chadwick's long shot made it 4-2 on fifty minutes, before Brady, Milward and Geary all went close to adding to the score.

It was therefore no great surprise when Chadwick added to his earlier effort, and at 5-2 any remote hope Burnley had was now extinguished. The away side did, however, reduce the arrears when McLardie got his hat-trick to make it 5-3 on eighty minutes.

With Everton fans reported in the *Cricket and Football Field* as chanting 'we want six', they duly got their wish when Chadwick crossed for Milward to push the ball home and, with two minutes remaining, the two again combined only this time Chadwick was the scorer – his third of the match. When the referee sounded the final whistle, Everton had won a truly great game by seven goals to three, and the sides were heartily cheered from the pitch at the end.

Sandy Lang

Full-back Sandy Lang was Burnley's first captain when League football came to Turf Moor in 1888. He was born at Bridge of Weir, near Paisley, in 1864 and was only twenty when he joined Padiham, then one of Lancashire's leading clubs, in 1884.

He was transferred to Burnley in 1885 and was a virtual ever-present during the early years of League football, becoming the first Turf Moor player to complete 100 League appearances in March 1893.

One of just two League goals that Sandy Lang scored in his senior career was Burnley's first-ever penalty in November 1891, after the introduction of the spot-kick the previous summer. West Brom were the victims in a 3-2 victory and Joe Reader, later an England international, was the goalkeeper on the receiving end. Lang retired from League football in 1895, joining Nelson, with whom he won a Lancashire League championship medal in 1896.

Sandy Lang became a publican in Burnley, but died tragically at his home in 1901, aged only thirty-seven.

Jack Keenan

A strong, powerful half-back, Jack Keenan came to Burnley from Clitheroe, his home town club, in 1884 and quickly established himself in a team consisting almost entirely of Scots. Keenan was a regular in his early days at Turf Moor, and his consistency brought him to the fringe of international honours. He was called up to join the England party in March 1888, but was not selected to play against Scotland in Glasgow, watching from the sidelines as England won 5-0.

He continued to be a regular choice in the Burnley side during the first years of League football, and was outstanding in the famous 2-0 Lancashire Cup final victory against Blackburn Rovers at Accrington in April 1890. Keenan retired from the game in 1893 to work in a local brewery.

Elsewhere
Derby 3 Notts County 1
Wolves 0 Sunderland 3

Monday 29 December
Bolton 6 Wolves 0

A Happy New Year
League Game 19
Thursday 1 January 1891
Everton 5 (Brady 2, Chadwick, Geary, Brown – own goal) *v.* Aston Villa 0
Venue: Anfield
Attendance: 9,000

Everton: D. Jardine, A. Hannah, D. Doyle, D. Kirkwood, J. Holt, C. Parry, A. Latta, A. Brady, F. Geary, E. Chadwick, A. Milward.

Aston Villa: J. Warner, G. Cox, W. Evans, J. Brown, H. Devey, G. Campbell, J. Cowan, A. Brown, W. Dickson, J. Graham, D. Hodgetts.

If Everton could win at home for the third time in six days, it would give them a big advantage in the race for the championship. After heavy frost in the previous few days, a thaw had reduced parts of the Anfield pitch to a boggy marsh and it was going to be a difficult slog for the twenty-two players.

The game began at a brisk pace, both sides forcing and wasting a number of corners with neither 'keeper troubled. Evans went close for Villa, but Jardine was out quickly to deny the opportunity. It wasn't until twenty-five minutes was on the clock before the first real chance in the game appeared, Chadwick driving the ball past Jimmy Warner to open the scoring.

Dennis Hodgetts was quick to respond, and ignoring the conditions he hauled himself and the ball past Kirkwood and Hannah, but as he shaped to shoot Parry was across in a flash to kick clear and earn the cheers of the crowd. Just before half-time, Jim Brown was unlucky when he headed Milward's cross past his own 'keeper. Everton thus ran off with a comfortable 2-0 lead.

Aston Villa were not finished, and on the restart looked to get themselves back in the game. Jardine was in fine form, though, and when Everton did get forward, Warner was forced to hurriedly kick clear, and when the ball arrived at Brady's feet he quickly struck it back past the 'keeper to make it 3-0. This was to prove the first of two in a minute for the Evertonian, the fourth taking the enthusiasm out of the Villa side and Geary soon made it 5-0, which was how the game finished.

Despite seeing five goals go past him, it was generally agreed that Warner had played well for Aston Villa and that he had been well supported by Gershom Cox, Billy Evans and Harry Devey. For Everton, Parry was felt to be the best of the halves; Jardine had done well to prevent Villa from scoring, but it was up front where they had been at their best, particularly on the left where Chadwick and Milward had used the dry ground to their advantage.

Elsewhere
Accrington 1 Wolves 2

James Cowan

Cowan spent fourteen years with Aston Villa, in which time he won five First Division titles and two FA Cup winners medals. A member of the famous Villa 'double' winning side of 1896/97, Cowan was one of the finest players of his generation. Remarkably quick, he once won the illustrious 100-yard 'New Year Sprint' event held at Powderhall. Parts of his winnings were used to pay a fine imposed on him by Villa for missing a game that day. Cowan later became the first official manager at Queens Park Rangers, where he led them to a Southern League title in 1907/08

Edging Nearer to a First Title

League Game 20
Saturday 3 January 1891
Everton 4 (Chadwick 2, Geary, Milward) *v.* Notts County 2 (Locker, Daft)
Venue: Anfield
Attendance: 12,000

Everton: D. Jardine, A. Hannah, D. Doyle, D. Kirkwood, J. Holt, W. Campbell, A. Latta, H. Robertson, F. Geary, E. Chadwick, A. Milward.
Notts County: G. Toone, W. Gunn, J. Hendry, A. Osborne, D. Calderhead, A. Shelton, A. McGregor, T. McInnes, J. Oswald, W. Locker, H. Daft.

With many matches having been called off because of poor weather, Everton took the chance to cement their position at the top of the League with a fourth consecutive (home) win. By doing so, they revenged their defeat at Nottingham, and ended any remote hopes County might have entertained of pipping them to the title.

In a bright opening to the game, Kirkwood had to be alert to block Harry Daft after a well-placed Tommy McInnes pass had opened up the Everton defence. Latta then shot past George Toone, only to find his effort ruled out for offside. The 'keeper, however, was unable to prevent the home side taking the lead on five minutes, when, after a great save from a Chadwick shot, he was let down by his defence who failed to react quickly enough to prevent Geary from prodding home the loose ball. The home crowd met the goal with great enthusiasm, and they were in fine voice soon after when Jardine produced a great save to deny Oswald an equalising goal.

The game was moving quickly from one end of the pitch to the other; Latta had a shot well saved by Toone, Daft then fired over and Andrew McGregor had a shot that missed narrowly. It was therefore something of a relief for Everton when Chadwick scored with a long-range effort. Yet this failed to dampen the away side's enthusiasm – Hannah and Doyle both cleared quickly and it was a grateful Everton side who ran off at half-time two goals to nil in the lead.

County continued to push forward on the restart, but by doing so they left themselves open at the back, Toone saved good efforts from Milward and Geary, before Daft again had Jardine scrambling across the box to push his shot away for a corner.

Everton's third of the game was a good one, Geary moving the ball quickly out to the left from where Milward moved inside to hit a shot which flew over the 'keeper and into the far corner. Daft however soon reduced the arrears before Everton quickly replied, with Robertson, Latta and Chadwick all giving Toone the opportunity to show just why he had been selected to represent the North against the South in a match that would decide the England side for the forthcoming England Home International Championship.

The Notts custodian had no chance, with Everton's fourth, Parry, finding Latta, whose quick pass was finished with a low drive by Geary.

Just before the end a McInnes pass to Bill Locker saw the Notts man make it 4-2, but at the end the home side had put themselves in a great position to become only the second side to win the Football League. Now only Preston and Burnley stood in their way. It meant that, at the end, their growing band of supporters cheered Everton to the dressing room.

Elsewhere
Blackburn 8 Derby County 0
Wolves 4 WBA 0

Prior to Game 21 Kick-Off Against Preston

Team	Played	Points
Everton	20	29
Wolves	20	26
Blackburn	17	22
Notts County	19	22
Bolton	16	17
Preston	14	16

Preston Prove Invincible
League Game 21
Saturday 10 January 1891
Everton 0 *v.* PNE 1 (Crossan)
Venue: Anfield
Attendance: 16,000

'The attendance was immense – with plenty of Evertonians but also a good PNE contingent added to by neutrals drawn by such a fine game.'

(*Liverpool Echo*)

Everton: D. Jardine, A. Hannah, D. Doyle, D. Kirkwood, J. Holt, C. Parry, A. Latta, A. Brady, F. Geary, E. Chadwick, A. Milward.

PNE: J. Trainer, R. Holmes, N. Ross, G. Drummond, W. Hendry, W. Stewart, J. Gordon, J. Drummond, W. Campbell, B. Crossen, H. Gallacher.

Everton kicked off knowing that victory would virtually seal a first-ever championship success. Thirty-one points would mean only Blackburn could overtake the Toffees, but to do so Rovers would have to win their remaining five games and hope Everton lost their final game of the season at Burnley. Victory for Preston would give the championship holders an outside chance of winning the League for a third consecutive year, and also open up an opportunity for second-placed Wolves to grab top spot by winning their remaining two fixtures. Everton were, therefore, in pole position, especially as they enjoyed a superior goal average compared to their rivals.

Kick-off time had been announced for 2.00 p.m., but long before that time the approaches to the ground were packed with people desperate to see the big match, and half an hour before the two teams emerged every available space was occupied, thus ensuring a record Anfield crowd.

There was a League debut for Bernard Crossen in the Preston colours, the Scot having been purchased from the great Scottish side Renton. Preston started the game kicking towards the Oakfield Road goal and Holt cleared desperately, as the away side looked to make a quick break through.

Considering the heavy snow of the previous week and the subsequent thaw, the pitch looked in fairly good condition, and there was some fine play down the Preston right which saw Jack Gordon force Jardine to make the first real save of the match.

Preston were playing the better football, and would have been much closer to the top of the League rather than in sixth place with just two away wins from six matches if they had been playing like this for the whole of the season. Billy Hendry's passing from centre-half was bringing his forwards into the play, and the Everton's backs had to work frantically to keep the away side from taking a crucial lead.

Crossen and William Campbell linked up to create an opening, with the latter's shot grazing the outside of the post to the relief of the home fans. Brady relieved the pressure with a well-hit shot but Bob Holmes was on hand to kick clear.

New Boots

Shortly after this, the referee stopped the game to examine a number of players' boots and Chadwick was forced to find a new pair. The break in action seemed to be just what Everton needed as, on the resumption, Geary and Chadwick both had shots at goal that George Drummond and Nick Ross kicked clear. Jack Drummond was then involved up front when, after winning the ball from Chadwick, his pass to Gordon saw his partner only just miss the goal.

It was to be only a temporary reprieve, as the *Cricket and Football Field* reported, 'The North End kept up the pressure, and from a long shot by Holmes a fierce scrimmage ensued in the Everton goalmouth, which terminated in Crossan's shooting through amid enthusiastic applause.' The goal was just reward for Preston's play, but stung by going behind, the home side surged forward. After Latta had floored Jimmy Trainer with a heavy shoulder charge, Brady's follow-up shot was hurtling into the goal, only for Holmes to prevent the equaliser by knocking the ball behind for a corner. Now it was the turn of Preston to defend deeply, Nick Ross was prominent with a number of good tackles and at half-time Preston lead 1-0.

Everton forwards made a rush on the Preston goal when play got back underway, but again Ross, to the cheers of the crowd, was on hand to intercept with a well-timed tackle. The referee was called into action when Holt and Campbell were involved in a dispute that seemed likely to end in fighting, and both men were cautioned. Trainer made a good save, but the best save came from the Everton 'keeper when Crossan's powerful shot threatened to double Preston's advantage.

The home side were now being noisily urged on by their supporters, but every time the Everton forwards did seem set to break through Nick Ross, captain of Everton in the first season of League football, was on hand and it was like there were three or four Nick Rosses on the pitch at one point. Despite their disappointment, the home fans were not going to ignore the Preston man's play, and he was roundly cheered on a number of occasions. Jardine then kept Everton in the match when he saved Gordon's drive.

With the game entering the last quarter of an hour, Everton made one last desperate surge, Milward was swapped to play centre-forward with Geary going out wide. Milward then forced Trainer to save smartly, but when the final whistle was blown Everton's title hopes had taken a blow.

There was at least good news for the home side when the result arrived from Derby where the home side had thrashed Wolves 9-0, a result that remains the latter's record defeat. With Blackburn not playing, the table was as follows:

Team	Played	Points
Everton	21	29
Wolves	21	26
Blackburn	17	22
Notts County	19	22
Preston	15	18

'Three teams could win the League – Everton, Blackburn Rovers and Preston.'

(Reported in *Cricket and Football Field*)

Elsewhere
Sunderland 5 Aston Villa 1
Accrington 2 Bolton 1
Derby 9 Wolves 0

Jack Gordon

Gordon had debuted in his teens for Preston while working as a joiner. He then returned to Scotland to play for Port Glasgow Athletic for two years. On his return in 1884, he quickly teamed up with Jimmy Ross down the Preston right and the pair were to prove a lethal combination. Against Hyde United in the 1887/88 season, the pair scored thirteen times in a record-breaking 26-0 FA Cup first-round success.

Gordon was lean and sinewy, his long legs taking him past many an opponent before he delivered a perfectly placed and weighted centre. In 1891, he was to become Preston's first scorer from the penalty spot and was to make his final of 113 League appearances against Derby County in November 1894, almost thirteen years after making his debut.

James Trainer

The Welsh international 'keeper joined Preston in 1887, and twice won the League with North End in 1888/89 and 1889/90. Capped twenty times by his country, where he often had far more to do than when playing for Preston, Trainer was to die in poverty in 1915, eighteen years after his 253rd and last appearance for the Deepdale side.

Everton Players in England Trial
Monday 12 January 1891

Everton players were well represented in the North side that played the South in an England trial match played at the Forest Ground, Nottingham.

The game saw the first official use of goal nets by the Football Association, and as they were made on Merseyside then it was appropriate that a player from there was the first to put the ball into them – Geary, scoring after quarter of an hour. The North doubled their lead when a Townley dribble ended with Chadwick making it 2-0, before Townley added a third just before half-time for the North. The second half saw the North remain in control and the South's defeat would have been much heavier if Wilkinson (Old Caruthusians) in goal hadn't played so brilliantly.

The FA Cup Until 1891

The FA Cup is the longest-running football tournament in the world. It kicked off on 11 November 1871, when eight teams took part in the first truly competitive football matches as a prize awaited the competition winners. The organisation behind it was the Football Association (hence the FA Cup) that had been formed in 1863 'with the object of establishing a definite code of rules for the regulation of the game'.

On the evening of 2 July 1871, FA secretary Charles William Alcock's proposal 'that a Challenge Cup should be established' was accepted, and the FA Cup was born. Alcock was to live to see the first Wembley final in 1923, dying aged ninety-three the following year.

The first final, at Kennington Oval, was contested between the Wanderers and Royal Engineers on 16 March 1872. Wanderers' success, the first of five, came from a single goal scored by Morton Peto Betts. Around 2,000 people paid 1s (5p) to watch the match.

In 1889, following the launch of the Football League that season, Preston North End became the first side to do 'the double', capturing the Division One championship and the FA Cup in the same season. Aston Villa joined them in the record books in 1897. It was to be another sixty-four years before a third side came around, Spurs winning both competitions in 1961.

Cup kings in 1890 were undoubtedly Blackburn Rovers, who had captured the trophy on four occasions in 1884, 1885, 1886 and 1890. Rovers' three wins in a row equalled that of the Wanderers between 1876 and 1878.

Dumped Out of the Cup

Saturday 17 January 1891 (FA Cup)
Sunderland 1 *v.* Everton 0
Venue: Newcastle Road
Attendance: 21,000

Sunderland: N. Doig, T. Porteous, J. Oliver, H. Wilson, J. Auld, J. Murray, J. Harvey, J. Smith, J. Campbell, J. Scott, D. Hannah.

Everton: J. Angus, D. McLean, D. Doyle, D. Kirkwood, J. Holt, C. Parry, A. Latta, F. Geary, H. Robertson, E. Chadwick, A. Milward.

Referee: Mr Jope of Wolverhampton.

Umpires: Tillotson of Birmingham, Strawson of Lincoln.

The most keenly anticipated cup tie in the first round of the English Cup took place at Newcastle Road when Sunderland took on Everton. It was rather unfortunate that two such good teams should meet so early in the competition, and a further cause for regret was that Sunderland Albion were also at home in the cup. Albion's opponents were the ninety-third Highlanders, who in the normal course of events are a big attraction in themselves. Everton arrived on Friday evening and stayed at the Roker Hotel so as to be fresh and ready for the fray.

The heavy overnight snowfall on Friday could have threatened the game, but the home club had engaged an army of men to clear 6 inches of snow from the pitch on Saturday morning. By noon the ground was clear, and the turf underneath was in fairly good condition, so everything was ready for the match. An inspection by club officials and the referee confirmed that the cup tie could go ahead. Jardine was absent for Everton and Angus was between the sticks. The NE railway company ran excursion trains from all over the district and all were well patronised.

From about 1 p.m. a steady stream of people made their way to the ground and the stands were soon crowded. There were seven or eight entrances and the gatemen were kept busy collecting money until the ground was full and people had to be turned away from the doors. The crowd was estimated at 20,000 and as the gate receipts were in excess of £420 it is likely that even more people were in the ground. Needless to say, it was a state of great excitement. A deafening noise greeted the teams when they appeared, with the large Everton contingent making themselves heard.

Everton won the toss, and Campbell kicked off playing from the road end. Play was in the midfield for the first two or three minutes, with both sets of forwards trying to force an opening only to be held in check by then half-backs. At last Harvie and Smith got away down the right, with Harvie's final shot going wide of the post. Then it was Everton's turn to get down, but Porteous and Oliver got the ball away splendidly and Auld sent the play back towards the Everton goal. Smith got in a shot that Campbell turned goalwards, only to see Angus make a fine save.

Sunderland returned again, and Smith and Scott both had shots cleared by the Everton defence before the visitors had a brief look in with Geary, Latta and Robertson making determined efforts to get past the home half-backs. Campbell checked the first try and then some good work from Murray kept Everton at bay. Scott and Hannah dashed away to be checked by McLean, and then nice passing between Scott, Campbell and Smith had Sunderland moving forward again; this time Holt stopped their progress.

Wilson latched onto the loose ball, and his powerful drive was only a whisker off target. Geary and Robertson had Everton on the attack again, and only fine work by Auld kept them out. A minute later the visitors got a free-kick, but Doyle's well-placed kick was booted away by Wilson. Everton were struggling to get into the game but a handball by Harvie took them into home territory. Auld's big clearance took the ball back into the visitor's goalmouth where Angus snatched the ball away from the onrushing home forwards.

Latta made a rush to the other end and fired in a good shot that Porteous managed to get away and sent Scott and Hannah racing up the left-wing. Hannah whipped in a snapshot that cleared the bar by inches. Milward got in a nice run for Everton, and when his pass found Chadwick he rattled in a beauty that had Doig at full stretch to save. Robertson was busy for the visitors and had beaten Auld, when Wilson stepped in and his challenge got the ball away. Doyle returned it but a free-kick to Sunderland had them threatening the visitor's goal again.

They were eventually repelled, and Latta went chasing after a long pass from Robertson. But Oliver got there first, and his big kick sent the ball well over the centre line. Milward came again for the visitors and had a good shot stopped by Doig.

Goal

Sunderland worked their way back into Everton territory, and a throw-in by Wilson was headed on by Campbell to Smith. He quickly gave Campbell a return pass and he beat Angus with a thunderous shot to put Sunderland ahead. Everton retaliated sharply and Doig saved his charge twice within a few minutes.

Oliver then prevented Latta from becoming dangerous, and Porteous stopped Chadwick at the expense of a corner as Everton searched for an equaliser. This was cleared only as far as Geary, but his powerful shot was off target. Oliver checked Geary again and then Robertson sent Milward dashing away and only a desperate tackle by Porteous rescued the home side. In the next minute a splendid shot from Latta flew just past the post, and then Doig saved superbly from Robertson and Porteous scrambled the ball out for a corner.

When this came over a handball, it gave Everton a free-kick close to goal, and when McLean crashed this into the net the visitors began to celebrate. It was premature however, for the referee ruled that the ball had gone straight through and awarded a goal kick. It was certainly an exciting moment, and home supporters breathed more freely when Doig sent the goal kick sailing away from the home goal. Sunderland raided briefly, but Milward and Chadwick broke quickly and passed to Latta who luckily for Sunderland was ruled offside.

The free-kick gave Hannah and Scott the chance to make a run with, Hannah's final shot being checked by McLean. Sunderland pressed again and Campbell sent one of his thunderbolts flashing over the bar. Scott followed this up with another grand shot that Angus saved, and then Campbell ended the attack by sending the ball behind. A foul on Scott brought Sunderland a free-kick and enabled them to press hard, with Murray and then Harvie sending shots wide. Campbell tried another cracking shot that brought a fine save from Angus and Murray put the rebound wide.

Oliver halted a run by Geary in fine style, and Murray stormed forward to bang in another shot that was wonderfully saved by Angus. He was challenged immediately by Campbell, Smith and Hannah, but cleverly sidestepped them and threw the ball away. Moments later the halftime whistle went. Robertson restarted the game and Sunderland attacked immediately, with Harvie collecting a pass from Campbell to fire in an effort that was cleared by Mclean. Soon afterwards Murray put in a long dropping shot that Angus fisted away.

Sunderland were at it again when Smith got possession right in front of goal, but somehow Angus got in the way of his cannonball shot and the ball rebounded clear. It was a marvellous save and deserved the applause that greeted it. The home side maintained the pressure and gave the Everton defence plenty of work to do but the call was answered well. A free-kick for a handball by Robertson was cleared, and then Campbell fired high over the bar from Smith's pass as Sunderland swarmed around the Everton goal.

The visitors were finding it impossible to get through, despite some clever work by their right-wing who found Murray in splendid form. Milward and Chadwick on the left made several attempts, but were no more successful against Wilson, who had their measure completely. At last after McLean had stopped a shot from Wilson, Robertson managed to show the way to the home goal and Latta put in a splendid shot, but he had wandered offside. The respite for Everton was only brief, and although they reached the centre line again soon after Murray promptly stopped any further progress.

Everton made another supreme effort and made several dangerous probing raids, but Oliver and Porteous were playing superbly and kept them at bay. Hannah got possession and set off on a run that took him half the length of the field, but under pressure from Kirkwood and Holt he ran the ball out of play. It soon became apparent that Everton had shot their bolt and Sunderland had little difficulty in holding off their feeble attacks. Sunderland however, was still looking for more goals and tried there hardest, but Holt, Doyle and McLean did sterling work for the visitors.

Time was fast approaching and the vast crowd were at such a pitch that when the final whistle blew they gave vent to the feelings of relief. Loud cheers rang around the ground and were repeated again and again outside the gates as the victorious Sunderland team returned to the clubhouse.

(Match report from *The Newcastle Daily Chronicle*)

1890/91 FA Cup

Sunderland were to make it through to the last four of the FA Cup, losing out to Notts County after a replay in the semi-final. The Midlanders' hopes of a first cup success were not to be fulfilled in the final, played at the Kennington Oval against Blackburn Rovers. On eight minutes, a Joe Lofthouse throw-in was never properly cleared, and George Dewar forced home the loose ball to the cheers of the Rovers fans in the 23,000 crowd, who together paid £1,454 to watch the game. Jack Southworth made it two on the half-hour mark and Billy Townley added a third a few minutes later. Notts County did reduce the arrears through Jack Oswald, but with the goal coming on seventy minutes there was never any real prospect of an unlikely recovery. The result meant that Blackburn became the first club to win the FA Cup on five occasions.

One-Month Wait Until Final League Fixture

Out of the FA Cup, Everton had over a month to wait before fulfilling their final League fixture. Intent on keeping the players fully fit – and on raising some much needed income – the Everton committee organised the club's first visit to the capital for a tour, which included three matches and kicked off against the famous Corinthian on 24 January 1891

N. Lane Jackson, who was dissatisfied that England had recently been losing to neighbours Scotland, had set up Corinthian in 1882. As the Scottish national team was mainly built of players from the amateur team, Queens Park, Corinthian was to be the English equivalent.

This set Corinthian apart from the other football sides of the time. Rather than play to win, they played to uphold their gentlemanly conduct by learning to control their temper, being considerate to opponents, battling to the end of the game, and being cheerful even after being defeated.

Despite the strict rules that they followed, including not playing in professional tournaments such as the FA Cup and later the Football League, Corinthian were initially hugely successful, They defeated FA Cup holders Blackburn Rovers in 1884 by a score of 8-1. Preston was defeated 5-0 a few years later. This success was set against examples of the 'Corinthian Spirit', and they refused to take penalties due to a belief that the opposition could not commit a deliberate foul, as that would be cheating. If an opponent was sent off, they would take a player of their own off.

Because they didn't play in professional competitions, Corinthian had a very open calendar and they filled it with global tours. It was these tours that led Real Madrid to adopt the Corinthian white shirts as their own, while teams from Brazil and Malta took on the Corinthian name, the Brazilian one being crowned Champions of the World for the second time in 2012.

Today, Corinthian Casuals ply their trade in the Isthmian League Division One South. Corinthian's 11-3 defeat of Manchester United in 1904 remains the Old Trafford side's biggest defeat.

24 January 1891
Everton 3 *v.* Corinthian 1
Venue: The Oval

Everton – Jardine, McLean, Doyle, Kirkwood, Holt, Parry, Latta, Wylie, Robertson, Chadwick, Milward.

Corinthian: Moon, Wells, Anderson, Winkworth, Brown, White, Brand, Currie, Lindley, Lambie, Sandlands – seven internationals.

Corinthian were missing a number of key players in Cotterill, Henfrey, Hossack and Ingham, all of whom were out injure, Everton were also missing Geary, due to a family bereavement, and Hannah and Brady, who still suffering knocks from the PNE game.

Poor weather and the doubling of admission prices to 1*s* (5p) meant there were only 2,000 present at kick-off. Robertson scored a cracker, but from the restart Sandilands showed great skill and speed and equalised within seconds. The game remained tied at half-time but in the second half Alf Milward scored twice to leave Everton deserved winners at 3-1.

26 January 1891
Everton 5 (Latta, Milward, Wylie, Robertson, Chadwick) *v.* Royal Arsenal 0
Venue: The Invicta Ground, Plumstead.
Attendance: 8,000

Everton: Jardine, McLean, Doyle, Shaw, Holt, Campbell, Latta, Wylie, Robertson, Chadwick, Milward.

Royal Arsenal: Bee, Connolly, McBean, Howat, Stewart, Julian, Christmas, Meggs, Gloak, Offer and Fry.

27 January 1891
Chatham 1 *v.* Everton 4 (Milward 2, Wylie, Elliott)
Venue: Park Lane, Chatham

Back home, Everton continued to play a series of games, beating Bolton 1-0 at Anfield with Milward the scorer. Further games brought the following friendly match results.

Sheff Wed 2 Everton 3
Everton 2 Bootle 1
Rotherham 2 Everton 5
Grimsby 1 Everton 5
Everton 2 Accrington 1
Blackburn Rovers 2 Everton 1

However, on 21 February came the much more serious business of the Lancashire Senior Cup. Away to Bolton Wanderers, Everton was thrashed 6-0 at Pikes Lane. The away side were at full-strength, but were 2-0 down at half-time and well beaten at the end. The decision by the selection committee to play Gordon and Wylie rather than Brady and Latta was heavily criticised in the following weekend's *Liverpool Sports Echo*. Bolton was to go on and win the competition. Everton finally got their hands on the trophy in 1893/94.

Revenge, of a sort, was swift. Back at Anfield the following weekend, for another friendly, Bolton went down 2-1. Then, on 7 March 1891, a benefit match for George Farmer, Alec Dick and Charlie Joliffe saw Everton overcome a spirited Darwen side 4-2 at home.

Alec Dick shares with Villa's Dennis Hodgetts the unenviable record of being the first player to be suspended by the Football League. The pair had clashed when the sides had met at Wellington Road in the early part of the 1888/89 season, and then Dick was also involved in an incident in Everton's away game at Notts County shortly afterwards. On 26 November 1888, Dick was suspended for two months and Hodgetts for a month.

Elsewhere
Saturday 24 January
Derby 2 Burnley 4
Preston 4 Aston Villa 1
Sunderland 4 Notts County 0

Thursday 5 February
PNE 7 Burnley 0

Saturday 7 February
Derby 3 Sunderland 1
WBA 1 Preston 3

Tuesday 10 February
Sunderland 2 Bolton 0
Notts County 4 Burnley 0

Saturday 21 February 1891
Preston 0 Sunderland 0

Wednesday 4 March
Accrington 0 Blackburn Rovers 4

Top of the League

Team	Played	Points
Everton	21	29
Wolves	21	26
Preston	19	25
Blackburn	18	24

Saturday 7 March
Blackburn 0 Bolton 2
Burnley 6 Preston 2
WBA 5 Accrington 1

Monday 9 March
WBA 1 Blackburn 0
Aston Villa 0 Preston 1

League Table at 10 March 1890

Team	Played	Points
Everton	21	29
Preston	21	27
Wolves	21	26
Blackburn	20	24

Off the Pitch – Jack the Ripper
A series of East London murders between August and November 1888 were the subject of newspaper coverage across Britain for a good many years afterwards. Jack the Ripper – a name that originated from a letter written

by someone claiming to be the murderer – was to escape justice. That didn't, however, stop people speculating who he might be and in the intervening years over a hundred suspects have been proposed.

One of these is James Thomas Sadler. He was a friend of Frances Coles, a prostitute murdered in Whitechapel on Friday 13 February 1891. Sadler had been seen with Coles earlier in the day, and was arrested on suspicion of murder by Chief Inspectors Donald Swanson and Henry Moore, with evidence suggesting they may have suspected he was the Ripper. Yet when it was quickly shown he had been at sea at the time of the earlier murders he was released without charge. No one was ever caught for Frances Coles' murder.

Champions Despite Last-Day Defeat

League Game 22
Saturday 14 March 1891
Burnley 3 (Haresnape, Bowes, Stewart) *v.* Everton 2 (Geary 2)
Venue: Turf Moor.

Burnley: A. Kaye, J. Walker, A. Lang, W. McFettridge, D. Spiers, A. Stewart, R. Haresnape, W. Bowes, T. Nicol, R. Marr, J. Hill.

Everton: D. Jardine, D. McLean, D. Doyle, A. Lochhead, J. Holt, C. Parry, A. Latta, A. Brady, F. Geary, E. Chadwick, A. Milward.

Referee: Mr C. J. Hughes of Northwich.

Having played impressively in the game against Darwen the previous weekend, Alec Lochhead, signed from Third Lanark in December, was given his League debut for Everton, the unfortunate David Kirkwood dropping out of the side. In fact, the new man was to play poorly, perhaps because he had not had time to develop an understanding of his fellow players.

Great interest centred in this match, the last of the League series so far as Everton were concerned, as the championship was partially involved in the issue. Over 800 excursionists travelled from Liverpool to Burnley, and when they arrived they found snow falling and the ground in a slippery condition with pools of water in places. The attendance was a large one, numbering about 10,000 and excitement very great.

Geary put the ball in motion and Chadwick went to the front, where Milward put behind. Latta ran down the wing in company with Brady who got round Lang, but without avail. Back went Latta and sent across, Milward again driving behind the goal. Jimmy Hill and Bob Marr then opened up the Burnley attack, where Lochhead deemed it best to send in to touch. This offered no check to the home left-wing, and McLean also kicked in to touch for which he was jeered. Burnley was persistent. Bill McFetteridge ran the ball out and then Doyle smartly arrested a strong raid.

The Everton left-wing relieved and, in trying to improve matters, Geary received a nasty kick on the knee, which seemed likely to render him *hors de combat,* but fortunately for Everton, he soon recovered. Burnley were driven back after a slight delay, the ball being sent to Kay by Sandy Lang and, from the custodian's kick, Haresnape got right down but shot wide. Parry cleared his lines and Chadwick and Milward worked beautifully and, became so threatening that Lang was driven to concede a corner. Everton attacked with much persistence for a long time, during which they won a number of corners.

Brady once put through, but was offside, and shortly after Geary tested Kay with a fine straight shot. Everton returned in taking style on either wing, but to no purpose. By means of long passes Burnley gained ground, but Doyle barred their progress, while Lochhead attended to renewed aggression. Latta soon dashed off, beating Lang and Kay ran out far to clear. Everton swooped down again and narrowly missed scoring while and Chadwick topped the bar, followed by a good aim by Geary.

Burnley broke of on the right in menacing manner. Doyle interposed by Hill came out strongly and called upon Jardine to stop a hard shoot. Some good work by Parry gave Everton an advantage, and for some time grand forward play harassed the Burnley defence. Hill, before any damage was done, raced off, and Jardine had to use his feet despite grand play on the part of Holt. Again, Lochhead failed to grapple with Hill and Marr and this led to a corner. Thus encouraged the home left-wing tried their luck once more, but Doyle when closing in stopped Marr.

Scoreless at Interval

A run by Geary was responded to by Marr, who seemed one too many for Lochhead, but found his peer in Doyle. A nice pass by Lochhead, however, atoned for past failures, and Chadwick forced Kay to fist out from a rasping shot, a performance soon repeated. The game tendered strongly in favour of Everton, the attack being well knit, but Kay saved out of the remarkable tough scrimmage, corners again being the order of the day. From now to the interval Burnley took up a strong position, but the Everton defence proved sound and ends were changed with nothing scored. On resuming, McLean at once dispossessed Hill and Marr and Everton took up the attack in earnest, and seemed certain of making a capture every moment of a sustained onslaught.

Two Quick Goals Increase Tension

Chadwick made a fine shot that was defended resolutely by Burnley, the ball bobbing in all directions about the goal. After Latta had returned and missed by a shade, Marr got within range. Jardine played the ball but did not put it far enough away, and so Bob Haresnape took full advantage by sending in a sharp return, and scoring a rattling goal.

Tremendous was the shout, which acknowledged this drawing of first blood but as the cheers subsided, Brady and Latta were away and Geary, getting hold, darted off and equalised in the Everton centre-forward's unique style, such a fine effort evoking a hearty cheer.

Everton Take 2-1 lead

McLean pulled up the Burnley left and gave to Geary, who ran down again, Lang checking him. Geary tried a shoot moments later and so did Milward, and the effort led to a hot scrimmage, out of which Kay was beaten for a second time. The ball coming off Burnley defender McFetteridge put Everton seemingly on course for the title.

The next incident was the unpleasant one of Parry being unceremoniously kicked, which caused him pain for the rest of the game. Everton seemed to have fairly broken up the Burnley formation now, and attacked so continuously that it looked only a question of how many goals they would win by, but after surviving many escapes, Burnley, some seven minutes from the finish, rallied surprisingly.

Equaliser on Eighty-Three Minutes

Hill led the way. Haresnape took up the theme and after Jardine had fisted out, he conceded a corner and from the tussle that ensued, Billy Bowes scored.

Burnley Rattle Home Their Third on Eighty-Five Minutes

There was but five minutes left, and on resuming, Alec Stewart closed in and beat Jardine with a high shot amid a scene of wild excitement. Latta made a good attempt to save the match. He ran down the wing and centred in to the goal, but Geary could not quite reach the ball and the game – a grand one – terminated in a plucky and sensational win for Burnley by three goals to two.

(Report from *Cricket and Football Field*)

The question was, had Everton blown their chances of the title? That would depend on the result at Sunderland. A 3-2 defeat meant Everton had a goal average of 2.17 (goals scored sixty-three, conceded twenty-six). A win for Preston at Newcastle Road would see them take the title on goal average if they won 1-0 (goal average 2.25) or 2-1 (goal average 2.19) but lose it on goal average by winning 3-2 (goal average 2.13).

Elsewhere
Sunderland 3 *v.* Preston North End 0 (Scott, Campbell)
Attendance: 5,000

Sunderland: Doig, Porteous, Oliver, Wilson, Gibson, Murray, Smith, Millar, Campbell, Hannah, Scott.

Preston North End: Trainor, Holmes, N. J. Ross, Kelso, Drummond, Stewart, McKenna, J. D. Ross, Raeside, Dewhurst, Gallocher.

Referee Mr Cooper of Wolverhampton.

Sunderland played their twenty-first game of the season when last season's Champions Preston North End visited Newcastle Road. Preston were a big attraction, and a crowd of 5,000 assembled to see this once-invincible team. However, many of the old brigade had departed and only N. J. Ross, J. D. Ross, Fred Dewhurst, Geo Drummond and Trainor remained. The weather was poor, with snow and sleet falling throughout the morning and although the ground had been cleared of snow, it was very soft and riddled with ruts made by the wheels of the carts used to carry the snow away.

Its appearance was depressing, and it was difficult to walk on let alone run. Sunderland was without Auld who was unfit and Gibson deputised. Preston arrived late on Friday night to ensure a good nights rest before the game. A nasty drizzling rain made conditions most unpleasant, and when Sunderland won the toss they decided to play from the road end. There was no wind and little advantage to be gained. Raeside kicked off for Preston and they rushed down immediately only to be beaten back by the home defence.

Sunderland got a free-kick and pressed, until McKenna came away for North End with a nice run down the wing. Oliver stuck with him until the ball went into touch. J. Ross received the throw and put in a shot that was blocked and after a minute or two of pressure around the home goal. Hannah dashed away and passed to Scott who drilled in a shot. Nick Ross tried to intercept, but the ball merely clipped his back on its way into goal to give Sunderland the lead in the eighth minute. A spell of midfield play followed, and then Campbell broke away to try a shot that went behind off Hannah.

Sunderland pressed again, with the ball being passed right along the home front line until Smith swung the ball across. Ross cleared weakly and the ball dropped to Campbell who slotted a fine low shot past Trainor for Sunderland's second goal. From the restart, Sunderland forced a corner that Ross put out for another flag kick. North End got this away but Sunderland remained on the attack, until some nice passing between Raeside, J. Ross and McKenna had Preston attacking. The ball reached Gallagher whose cross was cleared by Porteous.

Raeside brought the ball down again for Murray to get it away. Campbell and Smith made a rush and got the ball to Millar who was fouled by

N. Ross, but the free-kick was easily cleared. Play was quite open with Kelso, Drummond and Stewart doing some good work for the visitors. After a series of shots that the defence dealt with, Campbell banged in a nice effort that Trainor saved well. Doig had a couple of long-range shots to deal with that gave him no trouble and then Sunderland moved forward again, with N. Ross checking Smith and Millar three times in succession before Holmes finally kicked out.

Smith got possession and raced away to find Campbell with a fine centre, but Ross intercepted his pass to Millar. Scott got away again to whip in another good centre that Hannah helped on to Millar, who fired in a rasping shot that brought a brilliant save from Trainor. The corner was fruitless but the Preston defence was sorely tested with Bob Kelso and Nick Ross outstanding. A clever move between Scott, Campbell and Millar ended with Hannah banging the ball over the bar, and when North End responded McKenna ran the ball into touch.

Ross repelled Campbell at the other end, but he regained possession and got the ball to Millar. Millar passed to Hannah, whose shot beat Trainor, but was disallowed for offside. Raeside raided for Preston, but Dewhurst failed to hit the target with his effort. Mr Sudell claimed a foul but when this was not given by the referee, the Preston umpire walked off and did not return. The visitors pressed hard and showed improved form with Gallagher shooting wide and then Doig saving from McKenna in the closing minutes of the half.

Millar had been lame during the first half and was two or three minutes late in resuming after the interval. Preston in the meantime had swept down on the home goal and forced a couple of corners that were of no avail. Scott and Hannah tried to break, but Holmes stopped them, and when they tried again N. Ross held them at bay until Campbell got in a cracking shot that was superbly saved by Trainor. McKenna raced away from Preston and got past Oliver, but Wilson stayed with him and eventually hooked the ball away.

Gibson secured and sent Scott racing up the wing, but a grand tackle by Kelso put the ball into touch. Preston raided again when J. Ross sent a shot flying over the bar, and moments later McKenna put a shot wide. A long kick from Gibson sent Campbell chasing up the middle, but Ross got there first to kick away. Some really good passing by the Preston forwards created a grand opportunity for Dewhurst, but he shot straight at Doig who scrambled the ball out for a corner that came to nothing.

Preston swept back into the attack, but the home defence were playing well and kept them out. Eventually, Wilson sent Smith dashing away and he found Millar. Millar's cross was met by Campbell who banged his shot past Trainor and Holmes to score Sunderland's third goal. Almost from the kick-off, Smith tried a long shot that had Trainor scrambling to save. Preston rallied after this and played for all they were worth, but the home defence was superb. J. Ross put in a couple of shots one over the bar and the other past the post.

In Sunderland's next attack Smith was fouled, but Wilson drove the free-kick wide of the mark. Smith and Millar came again, and when Millar's pass found Scott he shot the ball through, but was ruled offside. Doig saved a couple of times in brief Preston attacks, but it was Sunderland who were on top with Murray striding forward to send a long shot over the bar. Near the close Millar beat Trainor again, but was given offside and the game ended in a grand 3-0 win for Sunderland.

Remarks

One has not heard the last of Mr Sudell walking off the field and leaving his side without an umpire for the referee Mr Cooper felt it very keenly. A man of Sudell's experience should have thought twice before taking such drastic action especially as the referee's decision seemed correct. The game was a good one considering the condition of the ground but Preston are not the team they used to be.

(*The Journal*)

Post Match analysis on Burnley–Everton

That Everton should be beaten by Burnley, after having three quarters of the game in their favour, was a sad disappointment and came with so much surprise that it seemed difficult to reconcile oneself to the fact that Burnley had won. However, all will admire the courageous manner in which Burnley kept pegging away right to the finish. Here was an abject lesson in the merit of never faltering as long as there was any time however short, in hand, and in some respect the victory was deserved, though the opinion that the better team had lost found pretty general expression even among the Burnleyites.

It was a splendid game and hardly a more perfect one could be hoped for on such a field of play, where a thin and treacherous coat of mud covered the frost-bound subsoil rendering footing always uncertain. Both sides were heartily in earnest and each appeared to have undergone special preparation for this crucial test. With Everton victory made the championship sure for them independent of what Sunderland might do. But 'All's well that ends well' and Everton, though they would have added lustre to their shield had they won, are to be congratulated on attaining the League championship.

(*Liverpool Courier*)

There was an air of dejection escorting the Everton fans as they left Turf Moor and wended their way towards the town centre before making their way through the cobbled streets that led up to Bank Top railway station. Here they slowly filled the railway carriages that awaited them. Their excursion train then steamed through the Lancashire & Yorkshire system and halted, for a refreshment break, at Blackburn Station. The more clued-up members of the party immediately headed for the station telegraph office where they heard some welcome news. They discovered that their rivals Preston had been beaten at Sunderland and consequently, Everton were the new champions of the Football League. The excursionists, their spirits rejuvenated, resumed their journey back home to Liverpool.

Burnley – Turf Moor

On 17 February 1883, Burnley, just nine months old, played their first match opposite the Wellington Hotel, which is still standing today, at Turf Moor against Rawtenstall. As it sounds, it was a piece of turf surrounded by moors. It didn't take long for the club's pioneers to make it splendid enough to accommodate a crowd of 12,000 for the match with local rivals Padiham in March 1884, 800 being seated in a grandstand, with an uncovered stand along two sides of the field for 5,000 more and the rest being able to watch the football on natural earth banks.

The facilities were fit for a prince, and in October 1886, Queen Victoria's son, Albert, turned up with 9,000 others to take in the action in the local derby match with Bolton. This would appear to be the first time a football ground was visited by a member of the Royal Family. The patronage of Britain's most important family was important to a game still cautiously making its way into the world. The Royal Family had long enjoyed horse racing, and its members were known to enjoy playing golf and tennis, but less so football. Ancestors of theirs had, of course, banned the unorganised games of centuries past with more than twenty laws between 1314 and 1667 outlawing a game believed at times to be taking people's attentions away from practising archery skills needed to deter potential invaders.

Times, though, were a-changing, as was demonstrated on 13 October 1888 when the Prince of Wales (the later Edward VII) attended the Kennington Oval to watch the London Swifts take on a Canadian touring side in a 2-2 draw. By 1914, the popularity of football was such that King George V was the first reigning monarch to attend the FA Cup final where he saw Burnley beat Liverpool 1-0. And, of course, with the Royals attending football matches other notable members of society also attended so that once the FA Cup final was moved permanently to Wembley in 1923 it became both a major sporting and social occasion.

Burnley continue to play their League games at Turf Moor. In 1888 the loom town of Burnley and nearby Nelson had a population of close to 100,000 people.

14 March 1890
Aston Villa 6 Wolves 2
Bolton 7 WBA 1

> What was the reason for the defeat at Turf Moor?
> The players blamed Jardine. He certainly did not play up to the mark, but was not altogether at fault. There was poor defensive play and Jack Hannah was a poor captain as he allowed too much arguing by the players. Lochhead played poorly and should be allowed to play his normal position. Geary was brilliant, especially his goal. Nevertheless Everton's triumphs under Mr Molyneux's reign have been great, and with him as secretary their success will be greater.
>
>   (*Liverpool Echo*, 21 March 1890)

21 March 1890
Accrington 1 Aston Villa 3
Bolton 1 Burnley 0
Sunderland 5 Derby County 1

23 March 1890
Everton committee meeting.
It was resolved that Kirkwood and Campbell would not be re-engaged for the 1891/92 season.

28 March 1890
Bolton 2 Blackburn 0

Saturday 18 April 1890
WBA 0 Accrington 1

Final Table
All sides played 22 games. 2 points for a win, 1 for a draw.

Everton	29
PNE	27
Notts County	26
Wolverhampton Wanderers	26
Bolton Wanderers	25
Blackburn Rovers	24

Sunderland*	23
Burnley	21
Aston Villa	18
Accrington	16
Derby County	15
WBA	12

*Deducted 2 points for fielding an unregistered player

Medals Purchased

Everton Committee meeting on Monday 30 March 1891.

It was resolved that the Secretary order twelve medals from P. Vaughton and Sons as per sample No. 11 in 18 Carat Government stamped at 52/- each net – engraving extra.

International Honours for Everton Stars

Following their successful appearances for the North *v.* South trial match, there was no great surprise that Edgar Chadwick and Alf Milward were asked to take their left-wing club partnership into the England side in the 1891 British Home Championship. The debutants lined up alongside fellow Evertonian Jack Holt.

So certain were the selectors of beating Wales and Ireland that they elected to play both on the same day, 7 March. Chadwick, Holt and Milward were selected to play against the former at Sunderland's Newcastle Road ground.

On the Wales side, Charlie Parry was selected to support W. Hughes and H. Jones in the half-back line-up; the Everton player was to perform with distinction and helped keep the scoreline respectable.

Both were on the scoresheet in the first thirty-seven minutes, with Chadwick making it 3-0 and Milward 4-0 after earlier goals from John Goodall and Jack Southworth. Howell reduced the arrears to leave the result England 4 Wales 1.

With the 'other' England also beating Ireland 6-1, the stage was set for the championship-deciding fixture against Scotland, who had also beaten both Wales and Ireland.

The decider, played at Ewood Park, proved to be a keen affair. Determined to beat the Scots, the England selectors chose an experienced team that included four of the successful Everton side in Holt. Geary, selected for his second international, Chadwick and Milward. Holt was to perform brilliantly, especially in the second half as Scotland searched for an equaliser. The Scots had chosen not to select any player who did not take part in the trial games, and consequently they were missing a number of good players.

After winning the toss, England forced the Scots to kick against a stiff wind. A dashing Chadwick run saw the Everton man find Goodall, who finished in great style to give England the lead on twenty minutes. Ten minutes later, England went further ahead when Chadwick drove a powerful shot from 25 yards that Vale of Leven 'keeper James Wilson got his hands to, but couldn't prevent entering the net amid tumultuous cheers. At half-time the home side remained 2-0 ahead.

England's backs were in determined fashion when the game resumed. They needed to be as Scotland pushed forward, before England showed some lovely passing ability to frustrate their opponents. With fifteen minutes of the game remaining, Francis Watt reduced the arrears with his third goal in four matches for his country and after which England dug deep to record a victory that ensured they won the 1891 Home International Championship.

Further Everton Friendly Fixtures
Following success in the League, Everton's season was far from at an end, the following games being organised:

Ardwick 1 Everton 2
Everton 1 Wolves 0
Everton 3 Vale of Leven 0
Everton 3 Corinthian 0
Everton 2 WBA 1
Shropshire 0 Everton 3
Everton 1 Notts County 0
Everton 2 PNE 1
Ulster 2 Everton 4
Bootle 1 Everton 2
Everton 1 Queen's Park 1
Everton 5 Accrington 2
Everton 5 Birmingham St George 0
Everton 1 Nottingham Forest 1
Notts County 0 Everton 1
Blackburn Rovers 3 Everton 0
Everton 9 Blackburn Rovers 0
Everton 4 Paisley Abercorn 1
Everton 2 Moss End Swifts 0
Everton 1 Queens Park (Glasgow) 1

Liverpool Senior Cup Success

Everton reserves had beaten Bootle Wanderers 7-0 away in the Liverpool Senior Cup first round on 2 February 1891, and then overcome Prescott 8-0 at Anfield on 23 February 1891 to set up a place in the final against Bootle on 28 April 1891.

The following report on proceedings is from the *Liverpool Mercury*:

BOOTLE 1 EVERTON 4

The seventh competition by the Liverpool Association was concluded yesterday evening, when Everton and Bootle met in the final tie, as they did last year at the Hawthorn Road enclosure. The winners of the cup in previous years were: 1883 Bootle, 1884 Everton, 1885 Earlestown, 1886 Everton, 1887 Everton, 1888 Bootle, 1889 Bootle, 1890 Everton.

More interest was taken in the contest this year than in that of recent occasions, consequent on the fact the Bootle had met Everton three times during the present season and had been beaten on each occasion by a single goal margin only.

Again Everton, through injuries, were not enabled to put their best team in the field, and this had the effect of equalising more closely, the respective sides.

The weather was fine, with conditions generally favourable for a fast game, and there were about 6,000 present.

Everton: Angus, goal, McLead, and Doyle backs, Locchead, Campbell, and Kirkwood half-backs, Latta, Brady, Hammond, Chadwick and Milward forwards. Bootle: Dunning, goal, Lambert, and Cain, backs, Grierson, Hughes, and Dodd, half-backs, Morris, Kilner, Murray, Hasting, and Jamieson, forwards. Mr Roberts of Chester officiated as referee, and Messrs A. R. Hull and Lamont were umpires.

Hammond started towards the Hawthorne Road goal, but Bootle opened the attack. Morris, however, put a bad finish on some neat passing on the right by driving wide of goal. Everton went away on the right, and Chadwick put the ball across, where from a fine pass, Milward shot over the bar.

Everton continued to press on the left, and after Lambert had made some good clearance, Milward again raised the ball over the bar. Hughes contributed excellent work in midfield, with the result that Bootle harassed the Everton defence and during the attack, Kilner grounded Campbell, who was hurt, but not sufficient to cause him to relinquish play. Doyle missed his kick, but danger was averted.

Everton, after Cain had beaten the right-wing, scored a grand goal, Chadwick shooting truly from Campbell's pass.

Bootle went to the front immediately in strength. When Doyle administrated a check three times rapidly. Everton dashed down to which the home team replied and Doyle again defended well. Morris, however, got within range, and shot keenly behind the goal.

At the other end Cain was reprimanded for his treatment of Chadwick and from the free-kick placed backwards by Lochhead, Doyle was very near with a long, low arm.

Hastings improved the outlook for Bootle by smart running, and despite the interception of Campbell he was enabled to make a good bid for goal.

Play was fast, and the ball travelled rapidly up and down, the best attempt at scoring just now being a headed shot by Latta. When well down in the Bootle quarters, Grierson handled the ball, and from a Lochhead placed kick the goal was penetrated but the claim that Latta had touched the ball was vetoed. This mattered not for Everton, for Chadwick picked out of a scrimmage and scored.

Chadwick, Milward and Brady sent in magnificent shots, while Dunning saved from a grounding by Chadwick a moment later. Everton had much the best of matters from now to the interval. From hands against Lambert, Lochhead placed accurately, and the ball gliding off Hammond's thigh went through, bring the visitors score up to three goals to nil, which was the record of most determined play up to time.

Everton had a strengthening wind against them on resuming, but opened the attack with much gusto through no damage was done. Hasting got off from a throw-in, and forced McLean to concede a corner – the second of the match, but this was of no assistance to Bootle.

Latta next sent across the goalmouth, and the ball going out, Bootle attacked strongly for some time, during which, Lochhead and Doyle acquitted themselves splendidly. Energy was the watchword, and Everton had a turn. Chadwick and Latta each shooting well, while Brady was conspicuous in company with his partner, in frequently battling Dodd.

From a smart run down the right-wing the ball was centred, but Hammond stumbled, and elbowed the ball through thus nullifying a fine chance.

Bootle was equally spirited, and brought considerable pressure to bear from the left-wing. Jamieson beat the defence, and the ball striking the inside of the post, bounding through. Hammond took aim at close range without effect. Bootle laid siege on goal by means of very good play, during which Hasting shot in hard, but too skyward, though Everton rarely permitted their rivals to become very dangerous.

The next goal, however, came from the cup holders, as on Brady passing to Chadwick the latter parted to Hammond, who ran straight down from the centre and shot home cleanly, and scored about the finest goal of the game, thus making some amends for previous indifferent play. Subsequently, Hasting put through from an offside position, and a hard game resulted in Everton winning the local cup for the fifth time.

Medals and League Trophy Presented

The presentation of the League and Liverpool Cups and medals to the Everton team was made the occasion of a great demonstration last night at the College Hall Shaw Street when Mr John Houlding presided, and was supported by Mr Molyneux, Mr Jackson, Mr A. Clayton, Mr H. Heard, Mr R. Wilson, Mr Lythgoe and Mr Hull.

The musical portion of the programme opened the proceedings, Mr Eaton Batty commencing with 'Comrades to Arms', which was song with all the flush, which characterises this vocalist's efforts. Several of the Everton players now began to arrive, and as each one took his seat he was met with a round of applause. The next feature was the rendition of 'The Maid of the Mill' by Mr T. Barlow whose fine tenor voice was heard to great advantage … The first half of the musical programme being now completed Mr R. Wilson came forward and said his duty was a simple and a pleasant one – it was to present the League Cup, which had been handed over to him on Monday by Mr McGregor, the representative of the League, to Mr Houlding as their President. Everton had done its work nobly and he sincerely hoped they would never let it fall into other hands.

Mr Houlding than asked the various members of the League team who were present to come up the platform and as each mounted the stage the cheering was terrific.

Mr Hull, president of the Liverpool & District Football Association next presented the Liverpool Cup. He was proud that Liverpool had shown up so well in the great contest of the year and hoped that twelve months hence the English Cup would stand next to it. Mr Houlding said he received the trophy with great pleasure. Since the Everton Club had been started they had scored many brilliant victors, the crowing point was reached when they brought home the League championship. It was only by continued perseverance and pluck that this cup could be won. The committee had surprised him by the knowledge they displayed not only as regards the game but also as regards players. If a good player were to be had they would capture him, and when they had them it was their duty to keep them. In conclusion he said he would always do the best he could to assist the club.

(The Liverpool Mercury, 9 May 1891)

As the committee was of the opinion that the various players should receive a memento of the occasion, he had now the pleasant duty of presenting each one with a gold medal. Unfortunately, several of their best players could not, for various causes, attend. Holt had not yet quite recovered from the accident he met with. Hannah had gone back to his business in Scotland; Kirkwood was ill from influenza; Parry who was injured in the international match, was still in Wales; and Milward had gone to sea, but all well, would be back with them again on 1 September. Angus was the first to come to the front for his medal, and Doyle and Campbell followed him in quick succession. Latta, who came next, met with a tremendous reception and so did Chadwick and Geary.

In connection with the Liverpool Cup, Mr Hull presented medals to the following players: Angus McLean, Doyle, Campbell, Lochhead, Latta, Hammond, Chadwick, and R. Jones. The chairman then said it was intended on a future occasion to present medals to those members, who had played in the qualifying matches. After a few words from Mr Hull, the presentation proceedings closed, and the second portion of the concert was proceeded with.

Annual Meeting

The annual meeting of the Everton members took place on 14 May 1891, in the Hall of Liverpool College on Shaw Street, in the Everton district of Liverpool. Mr John Houlding (president) occupied the chair. Also on the platform were Messrs R. Molyneux (secretary), R. Wilson (treasurer), W. Jackson (assistant treasurer) A. T. Coates, J. H. Williams and J. Woodcock.

After the chairmen opened the meeting, the secretary pointed out the fact that the club had, during the past season, played more matches away than at home, this being a contrast to the previous season. He said that for the coming season the new men engaged were R. Kelso (late of Preston North End), J. Marsden (from Darwen), A. Chadwick (from Heywood Central) and S. Thompson (from Wolverhampton).

Mr Wilson then submitted his balance sheet. It showed that the club, at the end of the season, was £1,792 in credit. He moved that a balance of £500 should be should be set aside as a reserve fund to enable the club to meet any unexpected demands upon them. The motion was seconded and carried. Mr Howarth, a club member, moved that 'this meeting recommend the committee to vote from the funds of the club, a sum of £30 for the purpose of presenting a testimonial to Mr Robert Wilson for his past services to the club.'

He referred to the excellent management of the financial department by Mr Wilson, and said that this gentleman was fully deserving of some recognition by the members of the club. The motion was seconded and carried amid great enthusiasm.

A recommendation was made that dressing accommodation for the players should be provided on the ground in one or two of the houses at the rear of the grandstand. The committee, the meeting was informed, already had this matter in hand. The president and committee members were then re-elected before Everton Football Club, having won their first League title, took their break for the summer.

Football League Extended

Meanwhile, it was agreed by the Football League that the League would be extended. A sub-committee that was appointed to revise the rules had proposed expanding the League to three divisions of twelve clubs each, but at the League AGM it was agreed to keep the increase to fourteen.

This pitched the bottom four clubs – Aston Villa, Accrington, Derby and West Bromwich – in a re-election battle for six places, with Darwen, Newton Heath, Notts Forest, Stoke, Sunderland Albion (all from the Alliance) and Ardwick. Villa, Accrington, Derby, WBA, Stoke – Alliance winners – and Darwen received the highest votes and were elected into the League. Meanwhile, a minimum admission price was imposed at 6*d*, with concessions for boys under fourteen and ladies allowed.

Scotland had meanwhile set up their own League in order to ensure they could hang on to their better players who were being lured south for professional football.

The Final Whistle

The 1890/91 campaign has long since faded from memory, and nearly 125 years since its demise I have tried to bring alive the momentous events surrounding it and introduce the players who played for a British footballing institution – Everton FC.

Those who represented the club in 1890/91 became the first from Merseyside to finish as League champions. The side contained some outstanding footballers in Edgar Chadwick, Johnny Holt and Alf Milward. In Dan Doyle and Andrew Hannah, the champions had the finest pair of full-backs in the land. In midfield, Alex Brady was the first in a long-list of Everton midfielders with the ability to pick a pass and unlock an opposing defence. Featuring alongside these players was a talented determined group that denied Preston a third League title.

Although the above names may seem foreign to a relative newcomer to the Everton scene, they are as much as part of the club as the modern players who take the field are. One day the current crop will also have faded into memory.

Legends never die, and I hope that the reader feels I have done justice to the Everton side of 1890/91.

ALSO AVAILABLE FROM AMBERLEY PUBLISHING

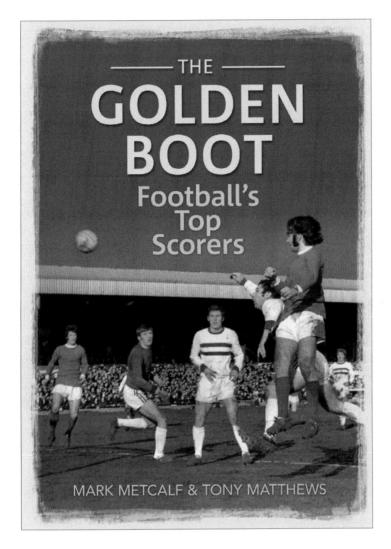

The Golden Boot: Football's Top Scorers

Mark Metcalf & Tony Matthews

The first history of the Golden Boot, from 1888 to the present day.

978 1 4456 0532 6
256 pages, illustrated throughout

Available from all good bookshops or order direct
from our website www.amberleybooks.com

ALSO AVAILABLE FROM AMBERLEY PUBLISHING

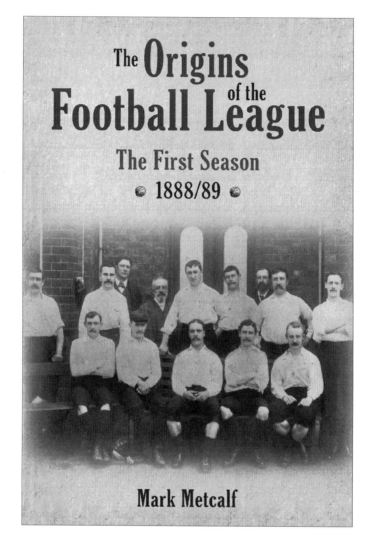

The Origins of the Football League
Mark Metcalf

Who actually scored the first-ever League goal?
For the first time, the history of the Football League's formation and
first season is told in great depth.

978 1 4456 1881 4
224 pages, 32 b&w illustrations

Available from all good bookshops or order direct
from our website www.amberleybooks.com